D1417174

What people are saying about …

Becoming Fearless

"I knew from the moment I met Michelle that it was going to be very easy to love her. What I didn't know then was how profoundly moved I would be by her journey, her courage, and her love for the Lord. I believe you will be too!"

Sheila Walsh, author of *The Shelter of God's Promises*

"Michelle Aguilar's journey is one of faith, endurance, and transformation. If you need both motivation and inspiration to get your life moving forward, you will find it in the powerful story of overcoming life's most difficult challenges and discovering God's best."

Jack Graham, pastor of Prestonwood Baptist Church

"As a *Biggest Loser* sister and a sister in the faith, I know Michelle's experience in facing her fears and trusting God for a deeper relationship is authentic. *Becoming Fearless* beautifully illustrates her journey in a tangible, easy-to-relate-to way. Through her honesty and inner evaluation, she echoes the sentiments in so many of our hearts and encourages us all to sacrifice in order to achieve our goals.

If you are looking for motivation to accomplish your wildest dreams, Michelle's book may be exactly what you need!"

Julie Hadden, speaker, author of *Fat Chance,* and runner-up on season four of *The Biggest Loser*

BECOMING Fearless

BECOMING *Fearless*

My Ongoing Journey of Learning
to Trust God

MICHELLE AGUILAR

David C Cook®

transforming lives together

BECOMING FEARLESS
Published by David C Cook
4050 Lee Vance View
Colorado Springs, CO 80918 U.S.A.

David C Cook Distribution Canada
55 Woodslee Avenue, Paris, Ontario, Canada N3L 3E5

David C Cook U.K., Kingsway Communications
Eastbourne, East Sussex BN23 6NT, England

David C Cook and the graphic circle C logo
are registered trademarks of Cook Communications Ministries.

"The Biggest Loser" is not associated with this book or any
of the views or information contained in this book.

The website addresses recommended throughout this book are offered as a
resource to you. These websites are not intended in any way to be or imply an
endorsement on the part of David C Cook, nor do we vouch for their content.

See Bible-resource credits at the back of this book.
The author has added italics to Scripture quotations for emphasis.

LCCN 2011933498
ISBN 978-1-4347-0327-9
eISBN 978-0-7814-0773-1

© 2011 Michelle Aguilar

The Team: Alex Field, Susan Tjaden, Nick Lee, Renada Arens, and Karen Athen
Cover Design: Amy Konyndyk
Cover Photo: David Edmonson
Family photos courtesy of Michelle Aguilar and the Aguilar family.

Printed in the United States of America
First Edition 2011

1 2 3 4 5 6 7 8 9 10

071811

For my family and friends …
Thank you for your love and support.
It's my prayer that you always seek
Christ first in all you do.
Proverbs 3:5–6

Contents

Acknowledgments

Writing a book is not a solo effort, and there are a number of people to whom I am indebted.

First, my parents: I am equally one half of each of you and cannot imagine being born into any other family. Dad, your constant love, support, and strength have allowed me the foundation to search for answers to all my questions. Thank you for never letting me give up or stop trying when you could see that I was so close to a breakthrough in my life. I am forever grateful for all the lessons you have taught me. Mom, our relationship has been quite a journey to get us to this place today; with all the ups and downs, I want you to know that I love you right where you are. God truly works in mysterious ways, and it has never been truer than during the last three years.

My brothers and sisters: Joseph, Drea, IAM, and Mia, I know we are affectionately referred to as the "fab five," but it's the four of you who have touched my heart so deeply. Your encouragement over our lifetimes has made such an impact, and it's created an unbreakable bond. Thank you for helping me keep this crazy life in perspective.

My agent: Lacy Lynch, thank you for being so patient as I learned this whole new world. I am so blessed to have our lives come full circle, and working together has been a true gift. Many thanks also to Jan Miller and Shannon Marven, CEO and VP of Dupree/Miller and Associates literary agency, for taking me on and laying the groundwork. You believed in the project.

My editor: Susan Tjaden, I don't know anyone who would want to be edited, but you have made it such a gentle process, and your encouragement has made all the difference. My cowriters: Sandy Bloomfield, your early dedication to this process was the perfect jumpstart. Thank you for catching the vision. And Amber England, who would have ever thought that all those coincidences would come in so handy? I cannot imagine a better way to get to the end of things. It's who you are when no one's looking that I admire most.

Pastor Jack Graham: I am honored to have had your support and belief that my story needed to be told, but thankful that it was not just lip service. Your effort to set all the wheels in motion is the marked difference in this book making it to the shelves.

My *Biggest Loser* trainer and friend: Jillian Michaels, it's said that people will forget what you say and what you do, but they will never forget the way you made them feel. While I have learned a lifetime's worth of lessons from you, it's the way you made me feel that will always have a special place in my heart.

Last but not least, my best friend and husband: Micah, your patience and kindness throughout this process has given us a stronger foundation, and I only love you more.

I know I'm filled to be emptied again, so God, the seed I've received from You I now sow.[1]

—Michelle

Foreword

When you think of John Wayne, surely a few things come to mind: American icon, *True Grit*, strength, and power. Well, when I arrived in Dallas/Fort Worth in the spring of 2008 to inform a mother and daughter they would be leaving the great state of Texas to join me on the campus of *The Biggest Loser* for an opportunity to change their lives, I wasn't expecting to find the female version of John Wayne. But that's exactly what I found the moment I met Michelle. She was full of spunk, to be sure, and proudly boasted a brave and beautiful smile—a smile that I would soon discover allowed Michelle to play the role of John Wayne to her entire family. But a smile that also served to hide Michelle's deepest fears and most gut-wrenching pain.

By season six of *Biggest Loser*, in which I and the rest of America would eventually grow to love Michelle Aguilar, I was less than optimistic about the intentions of the contestants who came to campus to change their lives, and my approach was probably, in no stretch of the imagination, "tough love" at its most brutal. So you can imagine the first conversation I had with Michelle wasn't exactly warm and fuzzy. It went something like this: "I'm not here to save your life. You have to do that yourself. I'm not here to be your friend."

Michelle responded with a straight face that didn't flinch. "That's fine—I don't need any more friends." Talk about true grit!

There was something about this woman that spoke to me. I knew that behind the John Wayne persona she had assumed back home, she was hiding a fierce inner struggle to find her own voice.

I was right.

The moment Michelle stepped foot onto campus and away from the comfort zone of being all things to all people back home, she began to allow herself to feel the pain of her past—the pain that led her to the place in her life where she was estranged from her mother and weighed a very unhealthy 242 pounds. The rough-and-tumble exterior quickly turned into a puddle of neediness—the very picture of anything but John Wayne. By week five, she was convinced she was ready to quit. As you may know, usually when someone I'm working with wants to walk out on their health, I let them. But with Michelle it was always different. I had asked her early on in a workout how bad she wanted to be on campus changing her life, and she answered without hesitation, "I want it bad!" And I believed her. So when she threatened to leave, I knew the pain she was feeling was working—and so I made a pact with Michelle: I would provide a safe environment for her breakdown, and she would lean into it.

Soon the work she was doing to shed her John Wayne facade and find her inner strength looked more like a scene straight from the Oscar-winning film *The King's Speech*—an unlikely underdog and an unorthodox coach determined to use any means possible to give Michelle a voice.

You probably already know that I use the gym as a metaphor for life. If I can create a situation in the gym that mimics a life obstacle for someone, and then get them to use their power in the gym to overcome that obstacle, I consider the beating I hand them a blessing. I recall a boxing workout with Michelle where I relentlessly swung at her face as she stood there sobbing and just let me do it. Finally, I stopped and said, "Michelle, if you want me to stop beating you, just tell me. Use your voice to set a boundary and tell me to stop."

Michelle came back with an ever-so-quiet, "My leg is hurting, and I don't think I want to kick today."

I pressed on. "SAY IT! MEAN IT!"

Her voice a little louder this time. "My leg is hurting, and I don't want to kick today!"

"OK," I said. "We won't kick today. I have to respect your voice."

Was Michelle scared to use her voice? Absolutely she was. But she never let the fear of using her voice quiet the rumble of greatness that was emerging from deep inside her. In fact, she went on to face many fears throughout her time on campus—many of which you will read about in this book—and was eventually crowned the champion of her season of *The Biggest Loser*. And at the end of Michelle's time on campus, she had not only emerged a winner in my heart but a friend for life. A smart, strong, and faithful woman who came to campus to face her fears and left having inspired a nation to face their own.

Let Michelle's journey to become fearless, written in the pages of this book, serve as inspiration to find your voice, to face your fears, and to trust that even when your journey seems long and lonely and too painful to bear, that you, too, have the true grit it takes to become all you were meant to become in this universe.

—Jillian Michaels, Michelle's
trainer on *The Biggest Loser*

Introduction

*"For I know the plans I have for you," declares
the LORD, "plans to prosper you and not to harm
you, plans to give you hope and a future."*
—Jeremiah 29:11

What are you afraid of?

If someone had asked me that question five years ago, I would
have said being caught without my makeup on or, heaven forbid,
showing up at church or work without the perfect outfit and perfect smile to mask my perfectly broken spirit. Today, I can finally
acknowledge that my true fears went far deeper than not sporting
the latest fashion trends to a midweek Bible study or showing
up to a dinner party without my hair coiffed to perfection. Fears
actually defined who I was: an insecure girl who looked to my job
for approval and identity, and who made it a point to keep friends

and coworkers at a safe distance so I could feel some sense of control in an often out-of-control world. Fear even distorted my view of relationships and responsibility, convincing me I needed to protect everyone around me—no matter what the personal sacrifice I had to make in the process. I feared letting people see the real me, and I feared letting outsiders see my real family because deep inside I knew we didn't meet the impossible image of perfection I had subconsciously set for all of us. Because we were in ministry, the bar was set high, and somehow I thought we weren't allowed to have any of the usual struggles families often go through. We are Christians, and to me that meant our greatest priority in life was to live a perfect life. It was all about setting examples and maintaining a respectable ministry image and living by the Golden Rule. Since no one else in my family seemed as preoccupied with these thoughts as I was, somewhere along the way I dubbed myself the bearer of the family honor.

Looking back now, I better understand the trap I fell into because I've found I wasn't alone in that trap. After several years of speaking about my experience on *The Biggest Loser*, I am amazed by how many others resonate with my struggle to trade my fear-driven survival for a life of fearlessness. Or at least fear-LESS-ness. I lived too much of my life in quiet denial, convincing myself that ignoring fears would make them go away—or at least recede far enough that I wouldn't have to deal with them. I wanted a perfect life so much that even as a kid I decided to go ahead and make one for myself. Anything that took place around me that didn't fit into my idea of how life should be I simply ignored or locked away in a drawer somewhere in the back of my mind. Determined to ignore the imperfections and chaos of my life, I put on my coat of armor—a perfect smile (with the help of a slight obsession with Crest Whitestrips), perfectly styled hair, and the perfect outfit—and got busy living my "perfect" life. Meanwhile, on the inside, I was a perfect mess and hoping against hope that no one would get too close and discover the truth of the secret I kept: My life and my family were anything but perfect.

But that was before *The Biggest Loser.*

In a cosmically ironic twist, the most fearful girl in the world ended up standing in front of America wearing only a sports bra and spandex shorts, letting it all hang out.

And that is where God decided my showdown with the fears that controlled my life would take place.

After years of running, with nowhere to hide and everything to lose, I finally turned to face my lifelong enemy: Fear with a capital *F.* I felt not unlike the trench-coated Neo in one of the pivotal scenes from *The Matrix,* when he finally decides to stop fleeing from the evil Agent Smith. One day, he simply stops running and instead turns to face the deadly foe that hounded and chased him for the first half of the movie. It is a dramatic moment of reckoning, and it all comes down to choice. Neo could have continued trying to live a step ahead of his fears, to appease and react the same way that he had all along, but that day he says no. Instead, he decides to face off against his greatest enemy and, in the process, simply becomes who he was born to be.

Similarly, a few weeks into the sixth season of *The Biggest Loser,* America's favorite reality weight-loss program, I could feel a crisis brewing with my old nemesis, Fear. I knew one of us wouldn't survive the experience, but I was not completely sure which it would be. When the moment of truth came, would I be able to make the right choice?

Could I become fearless?

Knowing Your Enemy

Fears are a lot like colds. There are many strains of each, and although they sometimes look alike, they're not. Think about it. Can you tell the difference between last year's cold and your most recent one? Or how about the way your heart pounds the same way whether you see someone lurking outside your window or are watching a killer inch toward the unsuspecting girl on the TV screen?

The common cold is viral in nature, and you never catch the same one twice since your immune system registers each one and produces antibodies to fight it in the future. Despite our body's best attempts at containing and disarming these pathogens, the system isn't as effective as you would think because the strains continually mutate, and new unregistered versions bypass the front line of our immune systems. If we are health fanatics and our systems are strong, we can greatly reduce the number and severity of colds caught—but no one is ever completely immune to them.

Fears, similarly, are viral in that they need an accommodating host to survive, can mutate into many forms, and can infect others easily. Even if we are emotionally healthy, we have to face the fact that we will never be completely immune to them—and that some fears are even necessary to keep us from ending up in dangerous circumstances. It's how we look at our fears and how we respond to them that determine whether they are stones that stub our toe or boulders that completely block our path.

Fear causes most of us to tighten up and brace ourselves, which in turn causes us to expect the worst and fall back into default patterns, shutting down our brains just when we need them the most. Have you heard of car wrecks in which everyone was killed or greatly injured except the drunks who caused them? They are usually the ones who walk away without a scratch. Those who fall asleep at the wheel also statistically fare better than average in the injury department. No, I'm not saying anyone should drive drunk or when exhausted. I'm only pointing out that alcohol and sleep cause muscles to relax—which, in general, turns out to be helpful in times of crisis. The impaired reaction keeps the body from tensing up to fight the impact of an accident and often limits the damage both physically and emotionally.

So what am I saying with all this?

That since we live in a world filled with both germs and fears of many strains and sizes, we will never be completely free of either. So we need to learn how to work with them. Every day gives us new opportunities to build up our physical and emotional immunity, keeping fears from paralyzing us every time we come up against them. In each decision, at every juncture or fork in the road of life we come to, we get to change everything that came before by what we choose to do in that moment. We can either sit in our fears and allow ourselves to be overwhelmed, as I did for so many years before being challenged by one of the tiniest but fiercest forces of nature on the planet—my *Biggest Loser* trainer, Jillian Michaels—or we can do as Jillian is known to say (or scream): *Feel the fear. Do it anyway.*

Sometimes, small decisions we make daily to confront our fears build the perfect platform to take the slower "tortoise" approach, and that's good enough for some of us to get where we need to go in life. Other times, it takes a single event or incident to bring all our old reactions and habits to a screeching halt, and open a new door to possibilities we may never, ever have thought possible this side of heaven. I was blessed that God orchestrated that very thing for me on a ranch in California, bringing me to the breaking point only to show me that where I thought everything was ending was where life would actually begin.

To say that the night I was crowned the winner of *The Biggest Loser*, standing on the giant scale with confetti falling from the sky, ended my battle with fear wouldn't be telling the entire story. It would leave the impression that somehow twelve weeks alone with my thoughts on *The Biggest Loser* ranch in California left me ten feet tall and bulletproof, without a fear in the world to overcome. That's the ending Hollywood likes to wrap up in a nice package with a big red (or in my case, pink) bow on top. To say I have conquered all would be saying I no longer need to trust God to work His will in my life as I face all the new challenges that each day brings. It's simply not true. And that is OK—and exactly how it's meant to be. I know I am still on my journey of becoming fearless, and it's in that journey where my faith in Him and belief in myself grow stronger every day.

Even writing this book challenged me to the core. Following *The Biggest Loser*, I felt pretty confident that I had just faced the most demanding physical experience the average person could expect to find in a lifetime. But the pummeling and scrutiny my physical body had endured for months on end was nothing—and I mean nothing—compared to the experience of having to write about what got me there in the first place. When I was first approached about writing a book, I remember being excited and even a little overwhelmed by the idea that people might actually want to hear what I had to say. But it wasn't long before I realized the emotional roller coaster I had agreed to climb aboard was by far more frightening than any beating Jillian Michaels threw my way. Baring my excess poundage to the world was no fun, but having to bare the deepest places of my soul and turn the light on areas that had been left unexamined for years brought me face-to-face with some of the greatest fears I have left to conquer to become the person I know God intends for me to become.

Through it all, I peer into the distance and see fearlessness beckoning to me as I take one shaky step at a time. I have learned to love "the becoming"—that in-between, sometimes messy place that connects who I was with who I know I really am and want to become. It's in this vulnerable, hanging-out-on-a-limb place that

I have learned to accept myself and rest in the fact that I am not defined by a scale or by someone else's expectations or by my past (and future) failures. Instead, I am defined by my loving heavenly Father, who declares me perfect in His sight and reminds me daily that I am limited only by my own perceptions. So I just need to stop giving so much attention and power to my fears and, instead, simply agree with what He already sees.

Are you ready to plow through fears, habits, and patterns that have sabotaged you in the past? You may never have the privilege of standing stripped down to spandex on TV as your weight-loss numbers are displayed on a wall like some kind of lottery game. But I believe that God has your moment or turning point waiting for you if (and when) you reach the point where the pain of what you're missing becomes greater than the pain of being paralyzed by the fears that come with change. It may be a dramatic event, like mine. Or you may be one of those "slow and steady wins the race" people. Either way, it all comes down to making choices that determine the direction of your "becoming."

I invite you to join me on my adventure, which includes insights and awareness gained from my once-in-a-lifetime experience on *The Biggest Loser* TV program. It took me from "little girl lost" to "champion crowned"—and allowed me the second chance that so many of us long for when we find ourselves stuck in one of life's many dead ends.

Fear is contagious. Fortunately, so is courage. Learning to become fearless will touch everyone around you, and best of all, you'll find it's a gift that keeps on giving.

1

Blindsided

Your pain is the breaking of the shell that encloses your
understanding. Even as the stone of the fruit must break,
that its heart may stand in the sun, so must you know pain.
—Kahlil Gibran, *The Prophet*

I stood at my filing cabinet that quiet afternoon, slowly clearing my desk of all the new folders and documents piled up there. It was only my second week at the railroad company in Fort Worth, my first "real" job following graduation. At eighteen, after a couple fast-food and retail positions, I was thrilled to have my very own desk in corporate America. The entire week had been a blur of information and activity, and it was good to finally be able to catch my breath and start winding down. I smiled and nodded at a coworker who walked by my office just as a call came through from the switchboard. I reached over and picked up the phone.

"Michelle speaking. Can I help you?"

"Hi, Michelle. It's Mom. Have you got a few minutes?"

"Sure. What's up?" Her voice had a strange edge to it, so I quickly straightened up and turned toward the window, away from the noise of the hallway.

"Well, I just wanted to call and tell you that I'm leaving your father. I've thought about it for a while, and I decided that things have changed and I need to move out. I've been packing most of the day, so I'm calling to let you know that when you get home for dinner, I won't be here."

All the air in the room disappeared, and for several seconds I couldn't breathe. *What?* It seemed like an eternity before I could form any words to respond to her. Finally, I choked out a feeble "What? … What did you say?"

If she began talking again, I couldn't hear her. My knees suddenly buckled, and I reached a shaky hand toward my chair, slowly pulling it out and collapsing onto it as my heart raced and my mind tried to keep the rest of my body functioning normally. There was simply no way my mother just told me she was leaving. I mean, how could she? As a mother, how could she choose to walk away from her children and not fight to keep the family she and my dad created intact? Even more, how could my family, a family so prominently committed to ministry work, survive the judgment those under our leadership would surely cast upon us?

"I'm sorry, sweetheart. I know this is hard. But I really can't stay. I just wanted to warn you first, since I haven't told your father yet, and you know how angry he'll get. I want to be out of here by the time he gets home."

"But … But why? What happened? Did you have a fight? Where are you going?"

My mind was trying desperately to place her words into some kind of context I could comprehend. Leaving? After over twenty years of marriage? I could not recall a single time either one of my parents had ever even mentioned the word *divorce*. My extended family back in California certainly had its fair share of broken marriages and relationships. But my parents were different. They had broken that cycle, or so I thought, and in my mind and in the minds of so many of my family members served as an example of what a loving marriage should be. Marriages didn't just end overnight—they usually eroded for years before something like this could take place, right? Things had been a little tense in our home recently, but certainly nothing that could have prepared me for this. Realizing that everything I'd believed about my parents' marriage and our family's life simply wasn't true crushed my soul. And to know Mom made the decision without giving the opportunity to ask questions, without a family meeting, left me feeling powerless and without a voice to plead with her to fight for us—for me. My mother continued calmly, talking as though she hadn't just ripped a hole in my heart the size of Texas and more as if she were calling to ask me to stop by and pick up a few groceries on the way home from work.

"No, it's not about anything specific. I've been struggling for a while, and I just need to be out on my own. You'll understand when you're older. I've rented a townhouse. Don't worry, I won't be too far."

She paused.

"Michelle, I'm taking Mia and Drea with me."

When would the bleeding stop? Seriously, how much more soul-crushing pain could she deliver in this one phone call that seemed to never end? Not only was my mother leaving, she was taking both my sisters with her and never once asked if I wanted to go too.

"What? Mia is only nine, Mom! Please don't do this!" My voice shook as I could no longer hold back the avalanche of emotions raining down on me, and my eighteen-year-old, try-to-hold-it-together self just lost it. I suddenly morphed from almost-independent adult to a four-year-old child unable to grasp the reality of life without Mom and Dad. And I began crying out like a child to my mother, "You can't…. Please, Mom, please—come home. You and Dad can work it out! Tell me what to do to help—I'll do it. Just don't leave—and please don't take Mia!"

I grasped at anything to try to hold my exploding world together. I had been raised to respect my elders and never speak to my parents in a disrespectful way, but what I wanted to say to her in that moment sounded more like this: "What are you thinking? You're the parent—you're not supposed to be messing up like this!

Why are you tearing our family apart, taking my sisters from me, from Dad, from their home? How dare you do this to our family?"

Andrea (or Drea, as our family called her) was sixteen at the time, and tended to lock horns with my dad a lot since she was the one most like him, so I wasn't too surprised that she would go with my mother. But Mia was another story.

When my mother was pregnant with Mia, I was eight, and I remember needing time to warm up to the idea that another baby was on the way. For so long it had been my older brother Joseph, me, and Drea—until IAM arrived. IAM, who was named after—you guessed it—God (my parents decided on his unusual name following the seventh in a series of inspirational trips they took to Israel), was still a baby, and there was nothing about this child that was typical. Somehow, even before he was born, my parents knew he would be different. They laughed for years about his dramatic arrival, where he literally flew out at the delivery and had to be caught midair. He was so much bigger than life right from the start that one babysitter for us kids wasn't enough. He needed his own sitter just to keep up with him. I got tired simply watching him tear around our house, getting into anything that wasn't nailed down. So when we found out that Mom was pregnant again, I was less than thrilled at the thought of another baby sibling.

That all changed in a heartbeat. Literally.

From the moment my baby sister, Mia, was born, and I gazed down at her beautiful little pink face and gathered the tiny bundle of softness into my arms, I knew she was beyond perfect.

I had always been the nurturing "little mama" type, but with Mia I took it to new heights, adopting her as my own and carrying my living baby doll everywhere I went. I bet her feet didn't touch the ground until she was almost four! We formed a bond early in Mia's life that still runs deep to this day. No matter how old Mia grows, she will always be my baby sister—the same tiny baby I fell head over heels in love with the second she was born.

And even though my precious Mia was growing up with an independent and adventurous spirit, I still had a unique bond with her. I couldn't bear the thought of having her ripped away.

In the blur of conversation during that phone call, I was filled with dread at what was about to happen to all our lives. I kept pushing aside and suppressing the overwhelming and completely unsettling question I had for my mother that was buried beneath it all: *"What about me, Mom? Why aren't you taking me? What is so wrong, so broken, about me that you aren't even asking me if I want to come with you?"*

As I struggled with the surface issues—the simple questions of who would get IAM to school and who would do the laundry and what about Sunday at church and what would that look like— something much more threatening to my sense of self-worth was happening deep inside. I had never consciously known rejection and abandonment issues before that phone call. But as my mother quietly announced that she was leaving me with my brothers and father for no reason that made any sense to me, that all changed. I couldn't shake the feelings of hurt and betrayal that crept in as I wondered what was wrong with me.

She never once asked me if I wanted to go with her. And that day my mother taught me an important, albeit destructive, lesson about rejection and protection: She rejected me before I could reject her. It's a classic psychological defense mechanism, and one she used without even realizing the lesson she passed on to me.

Now, I'm not saying that I would have left my father—I had always been a daddy's girl, and she knew how much I loved and looked up to him. But when she didn't ask me to come with her and took my sisters away, all I could think was that there must be something deeply wrong with me—I must have done something to make her want to leave me behind. And to carve up the family so neatly and not offer any choices (or even the most basic discussion of it) made the pain all the worse. Standing alone as the last kid chosen for a game of kickball in fourth-grade gym class was nothing compared to this. At least in kickball, you were eventually chosen. My mother never chose me on that day.

I had been working desperately to change my mother's mind and throw this whole awful conversation into reverse—to undo whatever was transpiring before it was too late. But I was getting nowhere, and the pain and stress left me running on empty. I had nothing left to give, so I finally gave up. At that point, I just wanted to get off the phone and forget this conversation had ever taken place. I wasn't finished at work. It was 3:00 p.m., and I knew I had to somehow focus to get through the rest of the day, so I grabbed my handbag and headed to the restroom to get myself together. In the hallway I ran into a coworker, a woman about my mom's age. Seeing my shaken expression, she stopped me with a gentle touch on my shoulder.

"Are you OK?" she asked with a concerned look.

That was all it took. I broke down and told her about the phone call, tears streaming down my face as I shared my terrible news. She assured me that everything would be OK, and that I could do whatever I needed to do. If I wanted to leave, I could do so without any problem. I thanked her and tried to compose myself as I decided what to do next. Trying to busy myself, but unable to do much of anything for the next hour, I decided to head home.

What would I say? What could I do? I wasn't certain where my mom would be, whether she would be finished packing or not, and I had mixed emotions about seeing her. She had hurt me deeply, and I wasn't sure I would be able to hold in the rage I felt in my heart for her that day. I got home to see my brothers and Dad carrying the last of her belongings out to the U-Haul sitting in the driveway. Apparently she hadn't made it out the door before Dad got home after all.

It was a scene I'll never forget. My dad—the loudest guy in the neighborhood and the man who always had the answers (even to questions nobody asked)—was strangely quiet as he carted the last of her things out the door and onto the truck. My mom had expected him to be out of control with anger at the news of her leaving, partly justifying her stealth tactics. But that day I saw a different side to my dad. Faced with this tragic moment, he didn't resort to anger or yelling. He wasn't dramatic or pushy. He just looked defeated, a man whose heart had quietly been broken in two. He finished loading up her stuff, and we all stood there as my mother got in and drove away.

As I walked back to the house, my new reality was waiting for me. Half of everything was gone. And I mean everything—even the sectional sofa had been separated into pieces! I was numb as I stood there, looking around at the wreckage of my family and home—almost as if a tornado had blown through and left a trail of destruction in its path. And not unlike the calm after a storm, all the noise and activity had given way to an eerie silence. I walked slowly back to my room, where I collapsed on the bed and began sobbing uncontrollably.

Like almost every other kid on the planet who goes through the trauma of separation or divorce, I felt somehow responsible for being unable to stop the demise of my family. I ran through countless scenarios in my mind—the tormenting what ifs and if onlys—trying to identify clues or warning signs that could help me make sense of my mom's decision.

Most of all, I wondered how life could go on now that half of my world had been packed up and put on a truck that was headed for the other side of town.

2

The Beginnings of Things ...

*There is an interconnectedness among members that
bonds the family, much like mountain climbers who
rope themselves together when climbing a mountain,
so that if someone should slip or need support, he's
held up by the others until he regains his footing.*

—Dr. Phil McGraw, *Family First*

It Takes a Village

In the process of writing this book, I ran across this passage from
Dr. Phil's book *Family First* and instantly fell in love with the

message behind it. I believe this passage embodies everything good not just about my family, but every family. To me, it perfectly describes what I experienced early in life growing up in California and even after the divorce: We learned to lean on each other through good times and bad, and that each of us was at our best drawing on the strength of our church family and on God's strength, love, and grace.

I can honestly say that most memories of my childhood days growing up in California are ones of complete happiness—plenty of love to go around, tons of laughter and practical jokes, and never, ever a dull moment. Raised around a host of loving grandparents, aunts, uncles, and cousins who served as a built-in network of loyal friends, I was homeschooled through my family's ministry in a place where we all lived near one another and did everything together. I was the middle of three cousins born a month apart, and we girls were inseparable. The saying "It takes a village to raise a child" rang true in my life. The village *was* my family, and in our village, we never lacked for companionship or adventure. My parents were on the leadership team of a church with close to five thousand people at its height (it grew quickly from our original congregation of two hundred that began in 1982). Everyone doted on us kids and went out of their way to ensure our every reasonable childhood want or desire was met. It was during this time my parents affectionately bestowed upon me the pet name *Blanche Neige* (Snow White in French) because, despite my Hispanic descent, my skin was ghostly pale and my hair was jet black.

Pastored by my uncle, who had accepted the Lord while in prison, our church attracted people from all walks of life, but specialized in ministering to the lost, the downtrodden, the rough-and-tumble ... including tattooed bikers, addicts, and the homeless—"the outcasts" of society that sadly many other more traditional churches wouldn't dare think of welcoming into their congregations. Despite some of the members having their fair share of rough edges and dark spots in their lives, these were some amazingly smart, resilient, and precious people who loved to worship the God who set them free from their chains of addiction and hard living. I remember taking such pride in one particular ministry our church was involved with. Our church partnered with the city of Anaheim in a special home-occupancy and rehabilitation agreement. Apparently many of the homeless people were setting municipally owned houses on fire in certain areas of the city, and in desperation, local officials approached our church leadership and asked if we would move in and oversee the vacant properties until the city could relocate the houses or rehab those who needed it. We happily did. Several of the homes housed people sent over by the state who needed a temporary place to camp out or regroup while struggling through an especially rough patch of life (which included folks representing every demographic from the homeless to white-collar workers in crisis).

The deep level of involvement in the ministry was a great setup, and my family thrived on the security and companionship of having extended family and friends nearby. In addition to being an associate pastor at his brother's church, my dad also oversaw a food and clothing bank. We grew up learning the importance of offering a helping hand to those in need—and solidified our family commitment to living a life that would reflect our close walk with Christ. Although there were certainly unique challenges, as our church took on some pretty tough cases of truly broken and lost souls through faith-based detox and addiction programs, we kids were spared the details to allow us our seemingly carefree existence. To us it was always summertime, and the living was easy.

An Unwelcome Unknown Arises

Not all of my childhood memories from California are fond ones, and looking back now, I have a better understanding of myself at that time. There came a day, as both my parents were working full-time in our family's ministry, when my dad needed to get a second job. He had gone through some testing for police work and was getting ready to go on the police force when a friend approached him about working at a YMCA. Already concerned about the dangers of police work, he thought about it and finally decided it was better for us kids if he took a job with lower pay but without the personal safety risks and shift work that comes with being in uniform. I believe my dad's decision to think of his family first was a selfless act and the right move in the long run, but that also meant we kids would have to leave the ministry's home-school group—which at the time was all we had ever known. To say I was devastated would be an understatement. I was crushed.

Despite the crying and the begging and pleading to my parents, they registered us in public school, and I was plucked from the intimate and informal environment of homeschooling (where there were five of us in a class) and suddenly surrounded by thirty other second-grade students at Adelaide Price Elementary School, where I knew and trusted not one soul. Even worse, I didn't know the routine of public school, and all the other kids were pros at it. It seemed that everyone else knew where to go and what to do, and I didn't. In the ministry, I had witnessed to the outcasts of society—now suddenly I *was* the outcast.

At first, my dad thought the new situation was ideal. Since the YMCA was right across the street from the school, he would be close by, which he knew was important to me. What he didn't know was that I was so distraught about this change that every day—between classes, at lunch (the cafeteria tables were outdoors because of the perpetual good weather), during outdoor PE classes, basically any time I could get away—I would head for the fence that enclosed the school yard and stand there crying my eyes out, hoping he would notice and come to rescue me from my own version of kid prison. Each morning I was a snotty, bawling mess as he dropped me off, and at any given time throughout the day the odds were good that he could glance out the massive picture window at the Y to see me clinging to the fence, staring longingly across the street, tears streaming down my puffy little face. I would watch for him as he worked with clients and staff, and if I was certain he saw me, I'd really let loose to make sure he knew just how miserable I was. Sometimes I would try to convince the crossing guard I needed to go see my dad, and other times things got so bad that Dad would get a call from the school office to come pick me up. I despised the entire situation even more since homeschooling had put me about a year ahead, so all I could think about was that I didn't even need to be there—I already knew this stuff! Many a Sunday night had me sick to my stomach as the hours ticked away and Monday morning's "dead man walking" routine started off another wretched week.

Needless to say, it was a long year for all of us. And at the end of the year, I had to enroll in summer classes despite my high grades because I had missed too much time due to absences and leaving early. As much as it pained me to admit this, it turned out that I actually enjoyed the summer session since the days were shorter and it was less crowded. But the shimmer of summer faded as the new school year drew near, and I began to get anxious, unable to stomach the thought of going back into that unknown, unfamiliar space that public school represented to me.

I pleaded with my dad to allow me to go back to school with my cousins. In a move that I now believe was a stroke of genius on his part (and one that taught me a powerful lesson I wouldn't fully understand until much later in life), he finally relented and said if I wanted to go back to the ministry homeschool, I would have to use my voice and ask my uncle. He knew this was a stretch and would throw me way outside my comfort zone because I was so shy. But that didn't matter to him. He put the ball in my court. My dad was teaching me my first lesson in becoming fearless at eight years old. I was scared to use my voice to ask my uncle if I could go back to homeschool, but there was no way I was going to spend another year crying my eyes out at the fence on the playground in public school. I mustered up the courage to call my uncle, and to my great relief, he said yes. So it was set—I would go back to our ministry's homeschooling program and nestle back in with my cousins until the sixth grade ... when my entire world would change.

The Move

When I was twelve, the ministry staff asked my dad to move my mom, me, and my brothers and sisters to Texas, where they needed Dad to oversee a ministry ranch. It was a tremendous sacrifice for my parents to leave everything they knew in California, including the comfort of our massive extended family and a secure job that my dad loved. Yet their commitment to the ministry and God ran deeper than all those things, and they never blinked an eye as we all packed up and headed to Texas. The agreement between my dad and the ministry would keep us in Texas for a year—but after that, we expected to move back to California, where we would go back to life as we knew it. At least that was the original plan.

We settled into our new home in the Lone Star State and enjoyed life on the ministry ranch. But just as the year ended, and we thought we would be headed west to California for our reunion with family and friends, my parents decided to leave full-time ministry. After a long road of odd jobs and trying to make ends meet, they both eventually took full-time jobs with an airline in Fort Worth. Looking back, I believe my mom and dad both viewed the move to Texas as an opportunity to spread their wings and fly as a family—out of the shadow of a large and successful ministry back home in California.

Today, I can see how that decision was honorable and rooted in the best of intentions to give my siblings and me a great life in Texas. Yet at the time, it was difficult for us kids. We had a huge adjustment to make, being apart from our family and friends. After we left the ministry ranch and my parents took jobs in the private sector, we found ourselves smack-dab in the middle of public school again—the very place that had crushed my soul as an eight-year-old in California. I tried to fit in as best I could. I even took up golf and lettered in the sport in high school. And even though I was able to get through the rest of my time in public school without the wave of emotions I displayed during my elementary years in Anaheim, I never felt as if I belonged there. I leaned heavily on my older brother, Joseph, for comfort and companionship at school and was ready to leave as soon as possible.

A year behind Joseph, I couldn't wait until I graduated. Well, actually, I didn't wait. Seeing Joseph edge closer to his final year of high school, I began to feel that familiar panic kicking in as I realized that would leave me without my older brother, who had become very much my protector. I couldn't bear the idea of navigating my senior year without him, so I went to great lengths to ensure it didn't happen. I took summer school and a correspondence class from Texas Tech University during my junior year to

earn the necessary credits to jump an entire grade—and I graduated right alongside Joseph.

Ready to Fly

With high-school graduation behind me, I was a little nervous
about the road ahead, yet excited about the endless possibilities life had to offer. I was eager to find my place in the world.
Following graduation, I decided to study aviation engineering at
our local community college. Since my parents both worked for
the airline, I thought it might be a natural move for me. I enjoyed
the semester and finished with great results. The success I had that
year was empowering, and it was probably my finest academic
accomplishment to that point. While I knew after a few weeks
that aviation engineering wasn't my life's calling, it was still a thrill
to know I could do it. I had used a wrench to break out of my
tiny, boxed-in world, but even then I knew there was so much
more to see and that it was time for me to move on and find out
what else life had in store.

After a few entry-level jobs in retail, day care, and the food
industry, I was excited when a friend connected me to my first
corporate job: working for the railroad. Of course, those unsettling fears of the unknown that I had experienced first at the age
of eight rose up in me just as I was getting ready for my first day
on the job. The surge of independence I had felt when I landed
the job turned into a gut-wrenching attack of nerves the closer my
start date came, and the night before my first day had me sick to

my stomach with fear. Inexplicably, I could feel my tears ready to burst through once again, just like my eight-year-old self on the public school playground in California, and it was all I could do to hold it together on the drive in to work that morning.

But I did it. I made it through the day without losing it, and the entire first week was pretty much without incident (unless you count having to call AAA to retrieve the keys I had left inside my locked car). Aside from some typical new-job jitters and the sheer exhaustion at the end of each day from the adrenaline rush that accompanies any new venture, I was well on my way. I took a deep breath and jumped in, and each day I grew a little stronger and little more confident—I was indeed finding my professional stride.

Each puzzle piece of my future slowly began to fall into place. I bought my first car, and then started putting money away as I looked toward the day I would get my first apartment. I was a bit giddy and felt empowered with this newfound path to freedom I was walking, secretly proud of each step as I began carving out a place for myself in this big world.

A month passed at my new job before the afternoon phone call from my mom that set my life on a completely unexpected path. But despite the turmoil in my personal life caused by my parents' separation, I somehow managed to find the strength to carry on. The day my mother left, I quickly stepped into the role she left behind as the caregiver of her children and the rock my father needed—the perfect picture of codependence, as I now see it. Drea would soon be approaching high-school graduation, and

Joseph was busy searching for his own independence. My strong foundation in my faith, which had been established early on in California, proved critical to my survival and personal growth during this time. I prayed to God for my family to be reunited, for my mother to come home, and for His will to be done in every aspect of my life—and patiently waited for His answer.

3

*A Prayer Answered ...
or So I Thought*

*Make allowance for each other's faults, and forgive anyone
who offends you. Remember, the Lord forgave you, so
you must forgive others. Above all, clothe yourselves with
love, which binds us all together in perfect harmony.*
—Colossians 3:13–14 (NLT)

April 6, 2002

*Well, God, where should I begin? So much has happened
in these last couple of months. I have begun to step way*

back.... I feel as though I'm finally starting to understand what it means to "let go and let God." I can only vaguely remember the exact words of my prayer, however, the feeling and sincerity of it have lingered with me, the desperation I was in—such sadness. Thank You for allowing me to cry out to You in the stillness of that night months ago. Your answers to that prayer—and the continuous ones since—have me in true AWE of You! How You work in such intricate detail is far beyond me.... I love You so much! I only hope that my lack of better words does not take away from how much I really do! ♥ May You keep my family safe and under Your protection. Let them feel Your love tonight as they sleep. In Your way, give them a hug from me. I love them! Be with me close as I sleep.... Let Your sweet warmth cover me from head to toe. Holy Spirit, please continue to quicken my heart for the right path that lines up with God's will for my life in the favored moments to come my way. Keep me from evil. Amen.

—Michelle's journal

I wrote this journal entry one blissful Saturday when I truly felt as if God had mercifully and perfectly fixed the broken places in my family's life. My mom had returned to my dad a year earlier after several months of separation. I was twenty now, and I had just stepped up into a brand-new role at a job that was filled with promise and challenge—a welcomed career path that was rooted in my passion for the creative world of television.

For the first time in ages, I was relaxed and enjoying every minute with my family as we spent the day at a friend's home. The sounds of fun and laughter ringing throughout the house brought a joyous smile to my face and healing to my battered heart. Being surrounded by my family represented my safe space, where I felt the most peace and where I believed I was at my finest. I honestly felt protected and cloaked in God's Spirit and fully embraced by His love and grace.

Rest assured, it wasn't a moment I took for granted.

After Mom left the previous year, I'd spent many sleepless nights with the weight of the world on my shoulders as I tried to find ways to fix the broken pieces of our lives. At various times, I would go over to her townhouse and beg and plead for her to return home and fix the brokenness that now defined this once-whole family. I would give each attempt everything I had—every ounce of energy in my body—as we went round and round about the situation. Wasn't her faith bigger than her relationship struggles? Weren't she and Dad the ones who taught us that divorce was wrong? Couldn't they just work through their issues together? What she was doing was so far off my radar as an option in life that I simply couldn't accept that she felt it was the only answer to the problems she was facing with my dad. Joseph would go with me when he could, and whatever angle I missed he tried. Despite our determined efforts—despite the tears, despite the hours upon hours of "Mom, please come home!"—neither of us ever seemed to get through. All that Mom would say to us was we didn't understand because we were too young and that we would one day when we were older.

And so, like many children—even adult children—who suffer separation or divorce fallout, I began to look deeper for some explanation for the unexplainable. I was convinced there must be something terribly wrong with me that caused the situation, or at least caused her to want to leave me, or that maybe I had made God mad, because no matter how much time I spent trying to convince her, she refused to come home.

After each failed attempt, I would cry out to God at night, begging Him to fix my broken family, and I would fall asleep sobbing and wondering why He was permitting these things to happen to us.

And then the miracle happened.

Following several months of shell shock and my trying to fill the hole Mom had left in our lives when she took the other girls and moved out, there came the stunning day when she returned. My parents began the daunting work of marriage counseling, trying to put the pieces back together again.

As relieved and thankful as I was to have her back home, it wasn't easy for me to just pick back up and carry on as though nothing had happened. After the initial flurry of excitement wore off, I found myself struggling with underlying feelings of mistrust, unforgiveness, and resentment toward her. I knew these issues weren't going to disappear overnight, even with all of us trying our best to readjust and settle back into a normal routine. We were never a family who wanted to unpack every aspect of the unpleasant reality we were facing—as if not talking about them would make the issues go away. We could be guilty of sweeping the ugly things under the rug, and that approach to my mother's return certainly didn't help matters. I had kept most of my thoughts to myself as I fought a lingering sense of betrayal and distrust, watching silently to see if my family would survive the wound it had suffered.

But through it all, I had some optimism and inner confidence in my family's resilience. I knew if we leaned on each other, relying on the family members who were strong in the moments when others were weak, we could bounce back. And here we were, over a year after her return, and we were getting stronger month by month as we kept moving forward together. We were really going to make it!

I glanced around the room, smiling at the silly fun my sisters and brothers were having and seeing my parents relaxed and enjoying the afternoon with our hosts. And in that moment, I finally felt it—a physical sense of release. It was as if I had been holding my breath without realizing it, waiting to exhale, and I finally felt safe enough so that I could. I leaned back and closed my eyes for a moment as I sent up a brief prayer of thanks to God, letting go of the last pieces of unforgiveness that had been keeping me from fully opening back up to my mom.

We were going to be all right. No, my family would never be exactly the same as it was before the split, but that was OK. We had made it through, and we would make it work and be closer as a family for it. I remembered reading somewhere that the place where a broken bone heals is stronger than the bone was originally. I knew that God would help each of us find our way through the multilayered process of healing, and we would be stronger. In three months I would be turning twenty-one, and the world suddenly felt like a brighter, happier place. That night, I picked up my journal and poured out my gratefulness as a new sense of hope filled me to overflowing.

That was on Saturday.

On Tuesday, my mother made the decision to leave for the second and final time.

My new hope, which had bloomed like the Texas wildflowers after a spring rain, died—killed by a winter frost that left a chill in my heart for years to come.

Dark Night of the Soul

With the new reality setting in that my mother was gone for good this time, my family split neatly down the middle. I felt as if I were walking with one foot on either side of a fault line, desperately hoping God would literally move heaven and earth to piece the two sides back together. Instead, the fault line erupted, widening the hole in my heart and the crack in our family. In order to survive the earthquake, I finally had to jump to one side, helplessly and powerlessly looking across the gaping canyon that separated my once-complete family.

Drea was away from home at college by this point. Mia had left with Mom the second time too, but returned home soon afterward. Mia's return was the only thing that got me out of bed on many days. I knew both Mia and IAM were at impressionable ages and needed a mother more than I needed to deal with my own feelings about Mom walking out on me. On many days, I wanted to curl up in a ball and hide in my closet because the pain was all consuming, but Mia and IAM deserved more than that, and I knew I had to deliver. So I would muster absolutely the last bit of strength I had in me to be all things mom to my baby brother and sister.

Shortly after Mom moved out and the divorce was final, we learned that she was getting remarried. *So soon?* It was almost too much to stomach—the pain of betrayal hit new depths, and my life began a slow spiral out of control. I remember feeling so hurt knowing she could move on so quickly after the years she had spent building our family with my dad. I was so mad at my mother on so many levels, I simply couldn't process the rage I was feeling in my heart. I had been raised to respect my elders—especially my mom and dad—but in that moment, when I looked at her, knowing how much her leaving had created a ripple effect of destruction in our lives, I simply had no respect for her.

After months of struggling with how to process it all, there came a day I told my mother that even though I still loved her deeply, the pain of interacting with her was too much for me to bear. I could no longer speak with her, and I had to choose to love her at a distance. And much as in the phone call when she explained she would be leaving Dad and never once asked me to go with her, my mother let me walk out of her life without fighting for me to stay.

I ended up loving her at a distance—our paths rarely crossing and not a single word spoken between us—for six long years.

Although I still loved God, I remember how the second departure caused something deep inside me to break—not just toward my mother, but in my spiritual life too. I began to pull back from God in fear as I wrestled with the purpose of faith and prayer in my life. What good were they if they didn't change the things in life that really mattered? How could He let these things happen? Why couldn't He keep my family from breaking apart? I quit going to church activities. In a way, I felt ignored by God and tricked by my mother. I felt kind of like Charlie Brown when Lucy once again pulls the football away as he goes to kick it, despite her assurances that it will be different this time and that he can trust her.

I even saw my rebellion show up in the guys I chose to date; I got involved in dead-end relationships that I knew had no chance. Although a little part was backlash and spite, it was mostly out of a need to feel as if I was controlling something in my life.

I had already done everything spiritually that I knew to do, but it had never seemed like enough, so I began to rely on myself.

I was doing it my own way. And I certainly didn't need any help from God—He had proven Himself just as unreliable as my mother.

Food took on a new prominence at this time. I always felt that I was a healthy kid growing up. I never considered myself "tiny," but weight was never a significant issue until after the divorce. In my efforts to self-soothe, I never saw the trap closing around me as the seductive comfort-relief cycle began. The guilt and shame that accompany overeating began to cover me like a heavy blanket, while unforgiveness and rebellion fueled my self-destructive eating binges. I began stopping at a convenience store each day on my way to work, then hitting a drive-through on the way back before dinner. Although I didn't fall into some of the patterns typical of overeaters, like hiding stashes of food around the house or at the office, I was a private eater. I began to be more self-conscious about my eating in public, choosing to nibble on salads or sometimes eating nothing when I was out at a restaurant with coworkers or friends. I saved my binges for when I was alone.

I remember looking in the mirror as the pounds began to creep on a few at a time, alarmed to see the changes taking place in my face and body as a few pounds of weight gain turned into one hundred pounds that completely overwhelmed my small frame. I was getting lost in myself and didn't know how to find my way back even if I wanted to. And I wasn't sure I wanted to. After all, the extra fat I was carrying served as a natural boundary to protect my heart, keeping people at a safe distance. If they ever got too close, they might hurt me.

Instead of turning to God and letting Him help me work through my pain, I backed away from Him because of my confusion over what felt like His lack of concern. I admit it became easier to relate to King David's confusion and withdrawal from God in 1 Chronicles 13:12. After years of a close and loving relationship with his Creator, David was shocked when God struck down one of his men, Uzzah, for doing what seemed like a good thing—trying to catch the Ark of the Covenant to keep it from falling to the ground (vv. 9–10). Everyone was thrown into a panic as they scrambled to figure out what happened, and despite David's love for God, his trust and expectations were deeply shaken.

I didn't want God's help because He had let me down. I wasn't going to Him with my daily struggles anymore because He hadn't fixed what I wanted Him to fix. I didn't trust that He had a bigger plan for me. All I could see was the pain, and I couldn't get to the other side of it. Occasionally I would wrestle with the decision to go back to God for help, but I would ultimately push Him away. I was spiraling out of control, yet all the while I knew deep down that God was there and that I should just let go and hand over everything. Clearly, I was making a mess of what was left of the situation, but I was stuck—I was too afraid and vulnerable to reach out. It seemed the further away from God I got, the harder it was to find my way back. I felt a strange fear and ambivalence toward Him—wanting Him to know I was angry and running from Him, but all the while hoping I wasn't so lost that He couldn't find me if I called out to Him.

And as the pain of my parents' situation got worse and worse and worse, I just got bigger and bigger and bigger.

As I wondered why God couldn't keep my family from breaking apart, I started to break apart myself—into two different Michelles, to be exact. The first Michelle was the girl who cried all the way to and from work, who became an expert at applying makeup in the car to hide the puffy eyes and red nose, who lived on breakfast burritos, M&Ms, and anything else that filled the emptiness inside. The girl who spent more and more time on the couch getting lost in the crazy lives of her favorite reality TV stars so she wouldn't have to take a hard look at her own. Taking care of two growing teens and a brokenhearted dad took its toll, and this girl hid the pain behind layers of insulation brought on by all the food—and she could never get enough.

The second Michelle was the girl with the pleasing ways and megawatt smile, who could outwork and outshine anyone as she climbed the corporate ladder and immersed herself in her career. This girl was unstoppable and always had the right answer to every question thrown at her because she knew the importance of image management and office politics. She kept just the right distance between herself and those around her—close enough to be friendly, but back far enough to keep them from discovering the chink in her armor.

These two Michelles would coexist for several years, until I was drowning in a depression so suffocating that I didn't want to breathe. I was barely able to keep a lid on the pain that accompanied me every single day of my life.

4

Navigating Relationships

*In God's wisdom, He frequently chooses to
meet our needs by showing His love toward us
through the hands and hearts of others.*
—Jack Hayford

It's funny how God works. He tends to show up in your life in
ways you simply can't imagine. While I was busy acting the parts
of two different Michelles, grieving the loss of my mom, playing
mother to my younger siblings, and consoling a brokenhearted
dad—all while trying to find my own voice and purpose in this

world—God used this time to fill in the broken places without my even realizing it. These broken spaces would be filled by a promising new career in television, a guy named Micah, whose own brave actions would inspire me to want more out of life, and an eventual boss and professional mentor named Karen, who truly took me under her wing and also became my best friend and most trusted partner in crime.

As I explained before, between the time Mom returned to the family and then departed again for good, I left the job at the railroad and took a job at a local television network. The opening at the network was in customer service, but I truly didn't care—I saw it as an opportunity for a real career. I had always been fascinated by television and wanted to learn the business. If it meant scraping gum off the sidewalk to get my foot in the door, then I would scrape gum off the sidewalk. Since my mother was home again at that time, it meant I could take a small break from being the glue that held us all together to step off my own professional branch and see if I could fly.

Despite my desire to fly, taking that step into thin air was daunting. We've already established that I don't process change and newness well, so while leaving the railroad job for an opportunity to learn the business of television was a no-brainer, it didn't come with great ease. Now twenty, with a few jobs under my belt and a sense of empowerment slowly blooming inside me, I still couldn't help but feel like that eight-year-old girl back in California who was panicked at the thought of starting anew among complete strangers. So the night before I started my new job at a local television network, I was sick to my stomach with nerves and cried and cried on my commute to work that first morning. Luckily I would cross paths with Karen, my eventual boss and mentor, shortly after my arrival at the network, and those fears and panic of being among strangers morphed into an eagerness to soak up as much knowledge as I could to climb the proverbial organizational ladder.

Things seemed to be progressing just the way I wanted at work—and at home, for that matter. At this point, my mom was still working on her marriage with my dad, and I was promoted out of customer service and into production after only three months at the television network. Thing were going so well, in fact, that it prompted me to write that journal entry in early April, when I gladly and humbly thanked God for the work He was doing in my life.

> *Thank You for allowing me to cry out to You in the stillness of that night months ago. Your answers to that prayer—and the continuous ones since—have me in true AWE of You! How You work in such intricate detail is far beyond me.... I love You so much!*

It still blows my mind that my mom left for good just three days after I wrote that journal entry. Thankfully, I had this new job filled with new challenges and a new boss, who would quickly begin to fill in the empty places left by my absentee

mother. In hindsight, I can see God's hand in all of this. At the
time, however, I didn't see the other set of "footprints in the
sand" alongside me. I thought I was alone and forsaken. I was
so embarrassed by what I had written to God in that journal
entry and felt so betrayed by Him that I was convinced He had
surely abandoned me—just like my mother. Had I simply run
toward the Word rather than from it, I would have discovered
the truth I had been raised to believe about my Savior: that He
never abandons His children.

> Are you tired? Worn out? Burned out on reli-
> gion? Come to me. Get away with me and you'll
> recover your life. I'll show you how to take a real
> rest. Walk with me and work with me—watch
> how I do it. Learn the unforced rhythms of grace.
> I won't lay anything heavy or ill-fitting on you.
> Keep company with me and you'll learn to live
> freely and lightly. (Matt. 11:28–30 MSG)

But run I did. My running away from God and my faith
didn't come in the form of addiction to booze or drugs or sexual
promiscuity or even being disrespectful to my earthly family, it
showed up instead by throwing myself into my career with reckless
abandon and keeping most people at arm's length. And although I
believe God brought Karen into my life for a reason, our relationship went from mentor-pupil to toxically codependent before I
could even begin to know how to turn things around.

My first few years at the television network now seem to be a bit of a blur. I had the opportunity of a lifetime, and I didn't want to blow it. Despite how bad things were at home—now that Mom was out of my life completely after I told her I would need to love her at a distance—I thrived at work. I poured whatever energy I had left from playing the role of John Wayne to my family into my role as an assistant director. And it was Karen who was there beside me, step-by-step, modeling how to be successful. I was in awe of how she took charge of situations with such ease, never batting an eye when it came time to make tough decisions.

But beyond that, what truly touched my heart was the way she genuinely seemed to care about me as a person. I was so fascinated by everything about her. She could throw a party unlike anything I had ever seen, she was a loving mother to her two children, and she was a supportive wife. She appeared to have it all together, and I wanted what she had. She would become my Yoda and I her Luke, both in our professional and personal lives. She knew my parents from their time in the ministry, and so it felt very natural to confide in her everything I was feeling about my parents' split. I told Karen things I'd never told anyone, and the trust I was able to place in her so quickly after losing all trust in women was baffling.

I was so enamored by Karen and so dependent on her that it became easy for me to turn to her—rather than God—when I was hurting or had lost my way. I completely ignored the Scripture that was buried in my heart:

But seek first his kingdom and his righteousness,
and all these things will be given to you as well.
(Matt. 6:33)

I absolutely wasn't seeking His kingdom first. And my life, both at home and at work, began to reflect it. My professional relationship with Karen, which started out perfectly innocuous—an eager new hire looking for a mentor and a very capable woman willing and ready to lead—had taken a turn in the wrong direction. There was an unhealthy level of codependence about it that both of us tried to ignore, but it just wouldn't go away. The boundaries between professional and personal started to blur, and I could feel both our work relationship and our budding friendship begin to unravel. But it seemed too much to bear. I couldn't lose another woman from my life—especially since I had stopped speaking to my mother after she left the second time. So I chose to ignore the unhealthy dynamic between Karen and me and continued to live in apparent bliss as the days ticked away.

A Boy Named Micah

With my relationship with my boss/best friend growing more toxic by the minute, my bond with my mother broken, and a job that had lost its luster, I was officially in a rut and needed a break from reality in the worst sort of way. Again, in hindsight, I can see how God strategically placed another person in my path at work who would come to play a big role in my life.

This time it was a guy, and I found him mildly intriguing. I say mildly because he was just grumpy enough to annoy me, yet smart enough that I wanted to know more about him.

He—Micah—came to the TV network as a freelance editor. He made such a good impression with the network executives that before long they offered him a full-time position, and he took it. Micah and I tended to lock horns more often than not, but despite the horn locking, there was a quality about him that I admired. Not only would he strive for the best in the show we were producing, it seemed as if he was somehow working to make me stronger ... better. I'll never forget how Micah encouraged me to find my voice. (Seems to be a recurring theme with me, doesn't it?)

We were putting together a segment for a show one day, and as the editor he asked me about specific details:

"Do you want this here, or that there?"

I stood there silently, unable to verbalize any kind of decision.

"Just tell me what you want, Michelle, and I'll make it happen."

And all I could muster back to him was, "I don't know. I mean ... What do you think looks good?"

He turned and looked me right in the eyes and said, "Michelle, you need to learn to say what you want. You have to be able to do that!"

During this time, work was rather demanding. The executives constantly wanted us to do more with less, and when my boss asked me to get more out of the production crew, I played bad cop and made it happen. I knew the demands I barked at them were asking a lot—oftentimes too much. But in the back of my mind, my only concern was keeping Karen happy and not letting her down, either as an employee or as a friend. I needed to stay loyal to Karen because I was afraid if I wasn't, and took Micah's side instead of hers, there would be hell to pay. (Translation: She would abandon me just as my mother did.) Micah knew the things I often asked of his crew weren't acceptable, and he would push back. I knew in my heart he was right, but I never let him know it—thus we were constantly at odds with each other as I served the role of buffer between him and my boss.

More to Life than Work

One day Micah came in to work incredibly excited about the band U2 announcing an upcoming tour date in Hawaii. Without really thinking, I blurted out that if he bought the concert tickets, I'd spring for plane tickets. After all, my dad worked at an airline and getting tickets was never difficult or expensive. A few weeks went by, and I didn't think another thing about it—until I found two tickets to the U2 concert in Hawaii lying on my keyboard at work. *Are you serious?* I sure hadn't been serious when I made the deal with him. It turned out Micah was a pro at putting his money where his mouth was, and so I was forced to do the same. I called my dad and made arrangements to fly Micah and me to Hawaii. And before I knew it, I was in paradise with this boy who totally annoyed me at work.

We would need some ground rules if this seven-day trip was going to work and serve as break from my crazy life back in Texas, so we made a pact—no fighting in paradise. And we didn't. Not one single argument happened between Micah and me—a small miracle all on its own! We simply relaxed on the beach, toured the island, watched the U2 concert, and took in all of that amazing place. There was nothing about this trip to Hawaii that was romantic between Micah and me—he was the ultimate gentleman and viewed me as a friend, and I can honestly say the same thing about my feelings toward him. There weren't fireworks. There weren't butterflies. Only a stress-free time and a much-needed reprieve from the crazy world I had left behind in Texas.

But I do remember thinking, *Wow, Micah and I get along really well outside of work. Who in their right mind would have thought this could ever happen?*

I also remember thinking how cool it was to want to get to know him better and be friends with him, not because I had to for work purposes, but simply because I enjoyed his company. We even ended up getting Hebrew tattoos on the last day of our trip in Hawaii—again thinking nothing of it. Everything was so simple and easy about that trip, and I felt at peace leaving the island knowing I had a new friend in Micah.

My respect for him deepened even more the following year. He came in to work one day, resignation letter in hand, and professed to us all that he was tired of "working for the man," that he was ready to be his own boss again, and would be leaving the network to go back to freelance.

Wow, I thought. *Here is a guy who believes in himself enough to walk away from a steady paycheck and reenter the crazy and unpredictable world that is freelance.*

I wanted to be mad at him for leaving me there amid all the chaos that seemed to be getting worse by the day at the station, but in my heart I was so proud of him and so admired his gusto that I couldn't be mad at all. We wished each other well and promised to keep in touch in the outside world.

I went back to being miserable at home and getting more and more miserable at work, while Micah went out and grabbed life by the horns without blinking an eye.

Coming Undone

With things in my work world pretty rocky, I was glad about one thing on the home front: Dad finally seemed to be coming out of the depression he had been in for the past few years. While my father and I had always been close, we had become even closer after Mom left—although it was a bond based more on shared loss than anything positive during this time. Dad was more open with his brokenness, and I did my best to support him as we tried to talk through it all. Finally, he seemed to turn a corner. The grief began to lift off him, and I was glad to see he was getting stronger. But something alarming began to happen.

At the same time when he began to pull out of the depths of his pain, I went into my own tailspin that I could not stop. I think that once I knew he was out of his own danger zone, it felt safer for me to take my turn hitting bottom. I lost my precarious footing and descended into some of the darkest moments of my life, when depression started to make way for thoughts of suicide and just wanting to end the thick blackness that was overwhelming me.

Driving home, so many times I would think, *If I just don't turn here where the road does, I can end it, and it will look like an accident.* There were nights of thinking, *This is it, this is as far as I can go.* But somehow, things never lined up exactly right. Someone would step in, the phone would ring, somebody would come home earlier than expected—there was always something to intervene or interrupt the plan. Looking back, I am grateful beyond words that God protected me from myself during that time.

Yet even at the lowest and darkest point of my depression, I sensed my faith hadn't completely left me because somehow I knew that I could still cry out to God and that He would hear me. He seemed so far away, yet I would think about the Scripture verse that tells how much He cares for the sparrow—there was no way He would abandon me. I just needed to figure out what was keeping me from letting go of the pain that was swallowing me whole.

So until I knew how to access the hurting places inside, I did the next best thing. I anesthetized myself on a daily basis with the one area I could control—what I put in my mouth. But soon the evidence appeared that screamed out to the world that I was anything but in control. The stress of living between the two Michelles was what caused me to gain over one hundred pounds in five years.

5

Daring to Hope

When you say a situation or a person is hopeless,
you are slamming the door in the face of God.
—Charles L. Allen, *All Things Are*
Possible Through Prayer

"Can you believe it? The open casting call is next week, and it's being held right over at Dave & Buster's on Stemmons. I got hooked up with a VIP ticket, so I won't have to wait outside in the heat with hundreds of other people.... And hey, Michelle—you should go too!"

I had stopped by my coworker's desk at the TV network after several days of feeling that I needed to check in and see how she was doing. I had finally made it over there to tell her she had been on my heart, and she immediately started spilling over with excitement about her latest adventure. I hadn't seen her so excited in a long time, and I felt a little jump in my spirit as the possibilities began racing through my own mind. We both knew we were perfect candidates for *The Biggest Loser* TV weight-loss program, each of us having passed the two-hundred-pound mark a ways back. We sure needed something to pull us out of the junk-food ditch we had fallen into—the only thing either of us had been losing recently was hope of ever seeing the 100s on the scale again.

"Wow! That's amazing! How did you get a VIP ticket? Maybe I should check it out …"

My sassy coworker smiled and shrugged her shoulders. "Girl, I guess I've just got the touch. I tracked them down on the Internet and sent them an email as soon as I heard they would be in town looking for contestants, and they contacted me right away to get some details. After I talked with them, I sent my story in, and they sent me a VIP, go-straight-to-the-head-of-the-line pass for this weekend! Isn't that awesome?"

I moved closer to the window that enclosed her work-space as she continued in an excited whisper with the details. Auditions for the fifth season of *The Biggest Loser (TBL)* would be targeting couples, and the program's casting staff planned to interview hundreds of obese Texans who would be gathering

next Saturday for this coveted opportunity. The show was set
to premier on the first day of 2008, with eight overweight
couples who would work with professional trainers for twelve
weeks as they competed for a cash prize of $250,000. I had
seen a few shows from prior seasons, and part of me wanted
to know more, but my more practical side questioned leaping
at the opportunity to bare everything I had spent years trying to hide on national TV. Yet the more I thought about the
idea of a lifestyle makeover, the more I warmed up to it all. I
had been drowning in pain and resignation for close to half a
decade—yes, it would be a huge leap out of my comfort zone,
but could this be my one chance to finally turn things around
in my out-of-control life?

Despite my initial excitement, there were a few obstacles to
get past first.

"Do you have a partner?" I asked my coworker.

"Yes," she replied. "I'm teamed up and ready to go!"

"Hmm. Maybe I could just go to the casting call and they
could match me up with someone there?"

"No—that's the thing, you have to come as a team. The relationship and back story is as important as how much you weigh."
Of course. Working for a TV network ourselves, we both knew
that it was always about what made for "good TV." It may be all
about a lifestyle change for us, but we couldn't forget that this was
ultimately about creating an unforgettable experience for millions
of viewers. And reality TV depended on the "wow" factor of a
handpicked cast.

I wondered who I should ask. I didn't have any friends who were as heavy as I was at this point, and even if I did, I would score a huge goose egg in the story department. I kept all my pain to myself, so very few people even really knew me, at least on a level that would be interesting to Hollywood. Except, of course, my dad.

My dad!

He was carrying extra weight on his short frame, and even though I needed to lose more than he did, he had plenty to work with. We would make a great team.

"Hey, I think I'll call my dad." I knew he would do anything for me. I had my cell phone with me, so I hit speed dial and he was on in a flash, listening as I passed along everything my coworker had just told me. When I finished, he said that if I wanted to do it, he was in. He promised me he would work it out and use whatever vacation time he had coming.

I thanked him and snapped the phone shut. "Dad said yes!" It had all taken less than two minutes.

Now, all I needed was that VIP pass and we were set. My coworker wrote down the info and I walked back to my desk, barely able to contain myself. Yet along with the excitement came those familiar nagging doubts. With my history of falling apart whenever I had to start anything new, I wasn't totally sure I could do this. Fortunately, I had been blessed with a dad who'd told me since I was a child that I could do anything I wanted to in life, so maybe it was time I stepped up and proved it to myself. Plus, he would be right there to support me in the process. Of course, with Dallas considered the chow capital of the nation with the most restaurants per capita (twenty-seven hundred eateries for one-and-a-quarter million residents)[2] this would be the perfect fishing pond for a weight-loss show. There would be all shapes, sizes, and stories trying for a place on *TBL's* tiny roster, and I knew it was a long shot. But I also knew what made a casting crew look twice at a candidate. And we had it. Besides a couple hundred pounds to lose between us, my dad and I had a strong enough back story of toughing life out together on our own to actually have a chance here.

I wrote to the name and email address my coworker had given me, and included some photos and a history of what had brought me to my current weight. I was shocked when later that same afternoon I got a call from their office. I was thrilled, but with only a few days left, I knew I had to work fast to get the VIP ticket in time. We talked for a while, and I answered all the casting staffer's questions. He seemed genuinely interested in my story, but as the conversation was winding down, I began to get a little anxious—nothing had been said about a special ticket or VIP pass. Had I overestimated their interest? Before we finished, he gave me directions and instructions to show up the following Tuesday, but my hope began to fade as I pictured myself and my father having to take our places in the huge crowd lined up in suffocating ninety-seven-degree weather. Ugh.

"OK, so I'm supposed to come Saturday and Tuesday—um, do I need a pass or anything?"

There. I said it.

"No." He seemed confused. "You're not coming on Saturday. Callbacks are on Tuesday, and I just told you I have you scheduled."

I almost swallowed my gum. Callbacks! Why didn't he say that in the first place? "Oh, right!" I said as calmly as I could. Forget the pass! We were in!

That evening, Dad and I were all over the details as we prepared for Tuesday. We were told to come ready to pitch our best to the network representatives, so we sat down and went over old (and still tender) ground as we synchronized our stories and talked through our best approach.

Later, he went to bed, and I walked over to my usual spot on the sofa and collapsed onto it, leaning back into the cushions and staring at the TV screen as I reached for the bowl of chips on the table next to me.

What if? What if I actually could have a shot at getting control of my life? What if Dad and I made it all the way to LA? We didn't need to actually win—it would be enough if we could learn some tips to lose just enough weight to jumpstart our own program at home. We didn't have to be the last ones standing, we just had to qualify to get out there and hang on long enough to slow this runaway train down!

I began to feel the anticipation rise. Somewhere deep inside, I knew that this was the chance I had never even dared to dream about—something that would finally be big enough to beat the depression that had been sucking the life out of me day after day. As my hand went back into the bowl, I suddenly lost my appetite.

I pulled away, smiling to myself as I got up and walked to my room.

On Our Way

Tuesday came, and we made it to the next round. We were well on our way to winning a spot at the official auditions in California. Within a few months, Dad and I were heading west. He had worked through a lot of red tape and gotten approval for the time off, while I had met with the top leadership at my organization, who agreed to release me for the "full monty" if we qualified. We had kept the news of our audition pretty well under wraps, and by the time we were on our way out to LA, we were both so pumped about our secret adventure we could barely stand it.

We got out there and settled into our hotel, planning to immerse ourselves in the audition process the next day and see how far we could go.

By the end of the week, and just one day until taping started, we were completely spent, having poured out our hearts in an intensive battery of emotional and physical tests. The tests were designed to flag any mental or medical issues and reveal any potential team player "ticking time bombs" that might go off at some inconvenient point later on in the season. After all, there's good TV, and then there's psychopath city—not exactly what the network execs are looking for. It was that day we discovered the good-news–bad-news scenario: Although we had not made the official roster, we were the first alternates. This meant that

if any of the teams were disqualified as the final results came in
from doctor exams and other last-minute details, we would be in.
Otherwise, it was *adios* and back to the real world.

Although we went to bed with no further news, unfortu-
nately our hotel room happened to overlook the *TBL* general
meeting room, where we had watched the teams come and go
throughout the week. As we saw the pairs assemble for the final
time that evening without us, we pretty much figured out that
we would not be joining them. We got up the next morning
to watch the bus pull away from the hotel, loaded with the
finalized cast of *TBL's* season-five players, all headed for the
Malibu ranch.

We received confirmation of the situation about the same
time, and even though we had already guessed the outcome, we
were still crushed. Despite our disappointment, we were amazed
we had gone as far as we had, and of course, were grateful for
the opportunity that few others had experienced. Shrugging our
shoulders wearily, we congratulated each other like the losing
team in the Super Bowl and packed up to go home.

It was over.

Changing Partners

The months that followed only cemented me deeper into my private hopelessness as I continued to live my double life—smiling
and perky at work, then falling down the rabbit hole each night at
home and covering the emotional mess with the temporary bliss

of cookies, pasta, sodas, and cheesy nachos. My dad would try to get me to go walking or to exercise—and I knew I needed to—but it all just seemed to take far more effort than I had to give. My tank was simply empty by the end of each day juggling a demanding job, which was bottoming out, my relationship with Karen, which was becoming increasing complex and messy, taking care of Mia and IAM, and doing my best to support my dad emotionally as we all inched forward in life.

After being rejected by *The Biggest Loser* for season five with my dad, I tried to settle into life again, but I was more miserable than ever.

I had been struggling at work for a while, and the atmosphere had begun to change. I enjoyed production but had realized during my time at the network that there were a lot of aspects to the work—including some office politics and drama—that I was not comfortable with. I also began to realize I wasn't cut out to be a "lifer" like others there, which caused subtle shifts in attitude, and sadly, tension began to set in. Remembering the feeling of pride I had when Micah boldly submitted his resignation to the network without any hesitation, I talked it over with my dad and told him I wanted to quit my job. Thinking he would tell me I should be more responsible than to quit a good job—a career, no less—and just suck it up and see if things turned around, my dad encouraged me to follow my heart. I'm not sure if you want to call it courage or just an overwhelming sense of being sick and tired of being sick and tired, but whatever it was that came over me, it was enough to muster my strength to write and submit an official

letter of resignation from the career I had created for myself at the
TV network.

I didn't have to wait long for God to orchestrate what was
next. Two days after I had given my notice, I got a call from *The
Biggest Loser*. They were putting together the next season's show
and were coming to town again. They had gone back over the
prior footage, remembering my father and me as solid contenders from the last round, and they wanted us to audition again.
I was stunned and flattered, but—remembering the gargantuan
amount of time and effort it had taken last time with nothing
but broken dreams to show for it afterward—had no intention of
going back for another try. I thanked them for their interest but
politely declined. At first, part of my reluctance to give it a second
try had to do with my need to forget frivolous pursuits like this
and focus on getting a job. I didn't think I had the time to do
anything but put my head in the classifieds and my energy into
resumes and interviews. And I had moved on after finally getting
all that "what-if-maybe-possibly-could-it-really-be-wow-yeah-
let's-do-it!" stuff out of my head and had a lot more important
things on my mind. It just seemed like too much wasted time,
trouble, and risk to try it all again. No—they could put another
set of gullible players through the wringer. This pair was finished.
The casting representative was not put off, though, and called me
three more times before I finally began to think seriously about
the possibility of going back. He assured me that he felt we would
have a great shot at getting on this time. After some back and
forth on the details, he finally convinced me to call Dad and talk

him into auditioning for season six, which, fortunately for us, would also be highlighting couples.

Against my better judgment, I began to feel the excitement kick in again. Part of me resisted, knowing the price Dad and I would have to pay without any guarantee it would turn out differently. Could I really risk pouring out everything just to get shot down again? But I couldn't help it—the dream was calling me back. I agreed to think about it, and called Dad after I hung up with *TBL*. Could it be that we were meant to do this after all? He picked up the phone, and I proceeded to share the big news with him, gaining momentum with every detail and laughing as I finished. I waited for his typical whoops of excitement.

Dead silence on the other end.

"Dad?" I asked tentatively. "What's wrong? Isn't this great news?"

He finally spoke. "Wow, honey, I would love to do it again, but I just can't. I only had enough vacation time for one shot at this, and there's no way I'll be able to get the time off to do both the audition and the program. And besides, this is Mia's senior year, and I really think I need to be here for her."

My roller-coaster ride had just hit both the highest and lowest points possible—all within the space of an hour. This was why I hated getting all excited about stuff—the big letdown was never too far behind and always worse than I expected. But I knew it was a lot to ask.

I sighed as I watched the dream die one more time. Of course I understood his job came first. I snapped back to reality and thanked him for all the time he gave doing it the first go-round, and told him I would call the casting manager with the bad news the next day. I needed to give myself a little time to get over the disappointment of it all. We chatted a little longer, and I was about to hang up, when I heard him say, "Wait—uh, Shelly?"

"Yeah, Dad?"

"What if ... What if you asked your mother to team up with you for this?"

This time, the silence was on my end. *What did he just say?*

He continued without skipping a beat. "No, really. This would be a great way to work on your relationship, and I'll bet you would both have an amazing time while you're at it. Think about it—how many people on the entire planet ever get an opportunity like this?"

I was still trying to wrap my brain around the idea of doing anything with my mom after having practically no contact at all for almost six years. I did know that she, too, had gained weight following the divorce. But there was too much we needed to work through together first. The implications were enormous, and I didn't have the energy or desire to begin to think of them all right now.

"I—I don't know—"

He cut me off. "Look, just think about it, Shelly. I think it's perfect for both of you, and who knows what God might be wanting to do in all this? Just sleep on it." I was amazed by his selflessness. Always putting my needs first, he was willing to step aside and allow—no, encourage—me to pursue this dream. Not alone, but with the one person who had hurt him the most in life.

As my dad's words bounced around in my head that night, the one thing I couldn't do was sleep. Should I really call my mom—when we were still struggling with baby steps back to any kind of real relationship—and ask her to be my partner for one of the most difficult physical and mental challenges of my life? Was that crazy? Was it foolish? Or was it possibly one of the best decisions I could make? Despite having kept God at an arm's length for so long, I prayed and asked Him to help me make the right move. I decided the answer to calling her was a resounding *yes.* I was filled with a peace and quiet resolve that washed over me, and I went to sleep with a plan to call in the morning.

All Roads Lead to Tiffany's

The next day, my stomach was in knots as I stared at the phone, willing myself to pick it up and make the call. What did I have to lose? If she said yes, we would both be so focused on what was ahead that we wouldn't have to worry much about small talk. If she said no, I would heave a sigh of relief and call them back to say "sorry," and then accept that it just wasn't meant to be.

There had been several years of a completely severed relationship, other than cards Mom would send with my sister Mia. She also sent little trinkets and gifts, but at the time, I was still working through my anger. All I could think was, *Really? You wrote me a card. I don't need a card—I need my mom.*

We began to communicate again on my twenty-sixth birthday, just prior to all *The Biggest Loser* auditions I went through with my dad, when she showed up at my workplace. But even that was pretty awkward.

The receptionist had called to announce there was someone waiting to see me in the lobby. I wasn't expecting anyone, and I remember the shockwave that swept over me with her next words.

"It's your mother."

Here? In my world? After almost six years, she decides to stop by? Feeling a queasiness settle into my gut, I knew I couldn't face her by myself. I immediately tracked down Karen and begged her to go with me. Mom knew Karen and had worked with her briefly in the past, so even though she didn't realize how close we'd grown, it wasn't so strange to have her with me. As we entered the lobby, my mother walked toward us, smiling, and handed me a small box.

"Happy birthday, Michelle."

After a hug and some slightly awkward moments, she nodded for me to open the gift, which turned out to be a beautiful "Return to Tiffany" silver heart pendant. Mom always had great fashion sense, and this was no exception.

The interesting thing about this particular necklace is that Karen, my "substitute" mom, was standing there wearing the exact same one—I had given it to her the previous Christmas. And if that wasn't bizarre enough, when Karen had given me a birthday gift earlier that day, she'd said she almost bought me the very same Tiffany pendant, which of course would have been on my neck when my mom came to visit.

At first I felt a strange sense of panic that Mom would see Karen's necklace and question her, so I decided to head that one off at the pass and pointed it out to Mom myself, although I didn't mention until much later that I was the one who had bought it for her. Karen fastened my new necklace on me, and we all chatted for a few more minutes before final embraces. Mom and I promised to meet for lunch, and we turned to go our separate ways back to work.

My mother and I began a tenuous walk together from that day—a text here, a phone call there—we even had a holiday lunch together. (I couldn't bring myself to accept her invitation to join her and her husband for Christmas dinner since it seemed as if that would be approving of her new life, which I was still struggling to accept.) We were moving forward slowly—but was I ready to take the step *The Biggest Loser* represented? Was she?

I took a deep breath and called her. She answered on the second ring.

"Hi, Mom. It's Michelle. I was wondering if you had a couple minutes to talk." She did. My heart started beating faster. Hearing her voice, I suddenly wasn't sure if I had thought everything through. I had secretly hoped for an answering machine to ease me in to this. But here we were. Before I chickened out, I just started talking.

"So, umm, you know how Dad and I were chosen as alternates for season five of *The Biggest Loser?* Well, funny thing, they called and asked us to be contenders for season six—an entire season dedicated to families. The only problem is, Dad can't go this time, and he suggested I call and ask you."

Clearly, trust was still a big issue in our relationship, and I couldn't open up my heart to her just yet. I couldn't tell her I wanted this opportunity to work on our relationship and that nothing would make me happier than a chance for a three-month reprieve from the real world to make it happen. Instead, I went with the safer option—letting her know in no uncertain terms that it was Dad's idea. I suspect we both knew the desire of my heart, and perhaps she was feeling the same apprehension, but if she was, her response didn't show it.

"Of course I'll do it. When do we leave?" Mom asked with the excitement of a four-year-old child on Christmas morning.

Although she had lost and gained weight with each of her five kids, she had gained most of her current weight following the divorce from Dad. So by the end of the call, we had both agreed to take the necessary steps that would put us on a path to ultimately fly out for the audition and quite possibly the full three-month commitment in California. She worked for a local church and was certain she would have no trouble getting permission for time off.

When I called the *TBL* casting staffer afterward, he was surprised but delighted with the unlikely turn of events. They knew my story from the last season, and the implications of our decision to do this as mother and daughter were nothing short of their ideal TV scenario. I could tell he wasn't quite sure what to think of my news—I could hear him flipping pages quickly to make sure that the mom I was now telling him about was indeed the same mom who had been off the radar for half a decade. (Yep. Same one.) We were a mother-daughter dream team as we planned for a shot at the grand prize and—more importantly—a new life for both of us.

Winds of Change

As I prepared for the trip west, I had a lot to think about. Not just what was ahead, but what I was leaving behind.

And as I pondered the whole scenario, I began to back up and look at everything with new eyes. I had been trying to push this "distraction" away in my effort to concentrate on my future, but I started to wonder if I had been missing the point—that this might be the door to that future. After thinking long and hard about it, and praying over everything, I felt that was, in fact, the case, and I decided to go with this new wind. Released from self-imposed hindrances, Mom and I plunged into the process— making videos, digging out old family photos, submitting written descriptions of our journey to this point—anything that would help paint the picture of who and what we would be bringing to the table. Time flew by as we completed our assignments for *TBL* and took care of all the details of our respective lives so we could be away for three months. I packed my things, and Mom and I flew out to meet with the casting crew, where we would do our best to capture a spot in the lineup.

The trip out to our home state of California was uneventful, as neither my mom nor I are drama queens by any stretch of the imagination. Add to that the awkward silence of strangers that we were experiencing with one another, and you can imagine the safe and superficial conversations we stuck to. We both tend to process emotions internally, putting on smiles for the outside world, while inside we might be the most miserable people on the planet. But the demands of living the life we did in the ministry—the need to appear perfect and strong in our faith—tended to keep the pain we felt inside, thus making for a very shallow existence. Besides, we were just beginning to grasp the hugeness of what we had agreed to, which in itself was plenty to chew on in silence. Each mile we flew took us deeper into a world that was as terrifying as it was inviting.

Once we got to California, we settled into our hotel room and began to mentally prepare ourselves for the week of auditions. Having been through the basic drill before and armed with a better understanding of what they would be looking for, I coached Mom on some of the nuances of reality programs and just prayed that we were both ready for this. She picked things up quickly, and by the end of the week we were exhausted, but felt we had given it our best. The rest was in God's hands.

This season was slightly different in that instead of going immediately on to the ranch, we were instructed to return home and wait for word of our acceptance or rejection. We were told we would have a camera crew going with us to continue videotaping our lives in preparation for the announcement of who had made it on to the season six cast. Although Mom and I were not given any more information on whether we were on the short list, my television background told me it seemed awfully strange to have an entire crew following us home if they weren't serious about us. I felt pretty good about our chances, although we were under strict orders not to tell a soul about any of it until we were officially notified of our acceptance.

Imagine my horror that Saturday night when our pastor called us to the stage to share our secret adventure with the entire congregation at Fellowship Church in Grapevine, Texas. Knowing the camera crew was at the back of the church, I could only smile big and cringe, thinking, *Oh great! We get this far, only to be disqualified because we couldn't keep quiet about it!* My mother worked at the church, so I figured she had shared some of the news as part of getting permission for the cameras to be there. Pastor Ed asked my mom a couple questions while I stood there, hands jammed in my pockets, wishing we could just melt into the carpet and be done with it. How were we going to explain this to the producers?

Then the pastor made a vague statement about a special guest, and suddenly a smiling Jillian Michaels, one of the *TBL* trainers, appeared out of nowhere and began walking up the aisle to hand deliver two pink T-shirts. Mom and I screamed at the same time. I was all over the place emotionally—overcome with relief that it was all planned and we wouldn't be knocked out before it began, and thrilled to my toes that we had made the final cut this time around. We were really in.

Mom and I were the official Pink Team for the sixth season of *TBL*. We were given a few days to pack and say our good-byes to our family, and then the day came for us to fly to California to *TBL*'s campus—"the ranch"—to begin our journey together.

And as fate (i.e., The Man Upstairs) would have it, that day we flew out to LA together happened to be Mother's Day—the first one in six years we'd spent together.

Let the Games Begin

The ride out to the ranch from our LA hotel was a quiet one since we were surrounded by other contestants, all of whom we were not yet permitted to talk to per our participant instructions. It seemed to take forever to get there (the ranch is pretty much out in the middle of nowhere) and upon our arrival, it finally began to sink in for Miss Control Freak here: I had just handed over my life to a production crew, which I would have absolutely no control over. At times like those, I wished I didn't have a background in TV production because I was suddenly painfully aware of the endless possibilities for our story in postproduction editing.

As assistant director for the network I had worked for, my role was to keep everyone on task and on time. Coordinating several production departments is no small feat, and you get used to playing traffic cop and making sure everyone is working in the same direction. To go from being the most important voice on set to being a cast member and having no say in anything felt pretty surreal at first. I was no longer a part of that team, now I was on the other side, being watched and recorded and shaped into someone else's idea of entertainment. I did notice that whether you are in a studio in Texas or on a reality show in LA, production crews are pretty much the same: The audio guys are still the best listeners you'll ever meet, the lighting guys are very detailed and particular about everything, the camera operators are always trying to figure out how to one-up each other, and the producers are looking to get inside your head. I knew that patience with the system would produce the best results, so I tried to settle back into the pace the crew was setting. Parts of our days were frantic and hurried, while other parts were like living in slow motion.

Once the show intro was taped and the first weigh-in complete, it was "game on," and we could all start talking with each other. Of course, that also began our introduction to the workouts, so very little talking happened until we all got back to the house that afternoon. For the other contestants, it was a thrill to be surrounded by all the lights and cameras. Their normal jobs were not bleeding into the experience as mine was, so they were experiencing it with new eyes, enjoying TV in all its packaged glory. The idea of being mic'd up and surrounded by so many people giving so much attention was fun for everyone but me, since for them it was like seeing beyond the curtain that I was usually behind. But I knew what was expected, and at the top of that list was getting a story. As someone who normally prefers to live completely under the radar, I admit there were moments when I questioned my sanity in agreeing to do this. Although I knew what I had gotten into, when it fully hit me that all these cameras and microphones were about to capture my every move for months, it was enough to trigger that familiar sense of sick-to-my-stomach panic and dread. I might as well have been starting the first day of the second grade all over again.

Soon the glamour of the set, crew, and atmosphere wore off, and we all became exhausted by the daily grind. Life on the ranch was more than just working out and eating—the television aspect was tough too. There were interviews and confessionals that took us away from the gym. The show's special events, called "challenges," pulled us off the set and into the real world, as many of them took place in public venues beyond the regular routine of the ranch. So much of our time was controlled by the show that we constantly had to make sure we were getting our workouts in as well as cooperating with the crew. Not everyone tolerated being jerked and ordered around very well; some of the players would come back from interviews pretty stressed out because it took too long or interrupted their workout. Time was so precious that being protective of it seemed natural.

The mental exhaustion kicked in early as well. On one hand, I was not alone in this experience. On the other hand, I was all alone. When we were finally introduced as the season six cast and taping had begun, the worst-case scenario happened. One of the hopes I had from the start was that being around so many other people would alleviate the pressure of being with my mom day and night. I figured we would probably make friends with the others on the show since we were all in the same boat and would have a lot in common. Yes, I knew it was a competition with only one grand-prize winner at the end, but I still expected that we would all settle amicably into our new world since on this show even losers were winners if we walked away with a new set of tools for living. How could we go wrong?

But it turned out that this cast was not made up of just any group of two-person teams. Although season five was made up of random pairs, the plan for this season was a little more specific: We were on *The Biggest Loser* "Families." Everyone was related, with the idea that four parent-child teams would compete against four husband-wife teams ("born to it vs. sworn to it"), which was definitely not what I was expecting. The party suddenly became intimate. I remember looking around at the group one time while we were waiting on the production team. Everyone was laughing with each other, hugging and leaning on one another with a comfortable ease from many years together. But while they all had a built-in support system (even if it hadn't always been a healthy support, since they were obviously one another's enablers), I couldn't help but feel like an outsider as I realized that I was the only player who had brought the source of my pain along with me. Furthermore, I had entered an official partnership with someone whom I had not been able to trust for over half a decade. And no matter how rocky the next few months would become, there was no going back now. Waves of fear washed over me.

However, if there was one thing these past six years had taught me it was this: Work hard, stay out of trouble, and just keep smiling no matter what—and no one will see how scared and lonely you really are. Little did I know that what had worked so well for me up until then was nowhere near what it would take to get me through the baptism of fire ahead. As I thought longingly of my confiscated cell phone and other broken connections to the outside world, the haunting words to the Eagles' song "Hotel California" kept running through my head.

> *"We are all just prisoners here of our own device."*
> . . . .
> *"Relax," said the night man,*
> *"We are programmed to receive.*
> *You can check out any time you like,*
> *But you can never leave."*[3]

Here we all were in California, each of us in our own private world of pain, and we were simply looking for a way out.

Ah, but that was my whole purpose in being here: not to just go through the motions of checking out, but to finally leave the comfort of my self-imposed physical and emotional prison once and for all. I wanted a bigger world than the one I had been living in, and I was willing to pay any price to get it.

Or was I?

6

Into the Fire

Practice is the hardest part of learning, and
training is the essence of transformation.
—Ann Voskamp, *One Thousand Gifts*

"Bob ... Jill ... they're all yours!"

With those words, *The Biggest Loser* host, Alison Sweeney, officially turned us over to our trainers, Bob Harper and Jillian Michaels, following the initial weigh-in. This season's theme was "Born to it or sworn to it," so each of the eight pairs of contestants would be assigned according to their status: Jillian would train all the family-member couples (born to it) while Bob would work with the married couples (sworn to it).

Most of us left there shaken up by the bigger-than-life weight numbers screaming at us from the huge board—numbers that we had gotten used to hiding or ignoring altogether. I had gone from 150 to a massive 242 pounds in five years, with an average gain of fifteen pounds a year. Now I would get to see how much of the damage I could reverse in a mere twelve weeks. And in the process, we would all learn for ourselves what makes grown men and women cry on this show. We left for our first gym session on the ranch warily, knowing that things would get worse before they got better. A lot worse.

From our first four-hour workout, we were immersed in the hurts-so-good world of Jillian and Bob, and we quickly saw we'd have to throw out anything that made sense outside these walls. I learned that having Jillian climb onto my legs and stand there yelling in my face as I leaned against the gym wall like a chair was perfectly normal in her world. As was her habit of threatening to dismantle body parts and use them as weapons to beat us. I believe her exact saying was: "I'll rip off your arms and beat you over the head with them if you jump off this treadmill." Ahhh … such love, huh? At our first outdoor challenge, I learned that hiking over a mile up a mountain in 110-degree heat was not considered cruel and unusual punishment, but rather a simple afternoon's work.

Because of all of the things we were juggling—workouts, food and water intake, TV time, planning for offsite challenges and events, training "homework," and sleep—we began to fear not only the grueling workouts, but the weigh-ins that were always just around the corner. Nothing could have prepared me for the kind of exhaustion we felt after our workouts, especially our first few weeks. I think for the first week I was in a perpetual daze, just shuffling from one task to another as my body was shocked out of its years of sedentary habits. In the gym, I prayed for two things: that I would get called out for an interview and (more than anything else) that I would not puke on camera. I wanted desperately to be able to make it through the workouts without puking for all the world to see.

Up until now we had been living on dreams, adrenaline, and the idea of change, but as the brutal realities of our commitment kicked in, we all hit our first wall—and a serious case of buyer's remorse. What had we agreed to? Would we survive this or instead be left in a sweaty heap on the gym floor with Jillian's voice the last thing ringing in our ears? "UNLESS YOU FAINT, PUKE, OR DIE ... Oops, looks like this one died. Move along, folks, nothing to look at here.... OK, everybody who's still alive, KEEP MOVING!"

We would have all dropped like flies the first day if Bob and Jillian hadn't kept propping us back up and driving us on. I recall the sheer terror rising in me when it was my turn to get off the treadmill and do some floor work with Jillian for the first time. All I could think as I walked toward her was, *Michelle,* whatever *you do, just* do not *upset her!* Jillian's legendary MO is to break people down so she can build them back up. If I had to compare the process to anything, it would be a broken bone that is healing improperly. The doctor has to break it a second time in order to set it so it will heal correctly. While the second break may be the right thing to do, the pain sure doesn't feel any different.

What took me by surprise was that when she met me out there on the gym floor, she didn't yell or scream. Instead, she got very quiet. Now, we are all a product of our experiences, and the only comparison I had to draw on was my dad. A normally loud, larger-than-life kind of guy, he would get quiet only when he was serious and had something extremely important he wanted me to hear. So, as Jillian zoned in and began to work with me, I listened to every word and did exactly as she said. Being able to focus on the training brought a sense of comfort, and I felt relief at the familiar style and clear instructions in the midst of so much chaos. Maybe this would work out after all.

Still, things were moving at a rapid pace. With the jubilant, rah-rah beginning a distant memory, I was just now noticing that the tiger I had grabbed by the tail was getting ready to turn and pounce. But it was too late to let go, so I took a deep breath, tightened my grip, and decided to hold on for the ride as long as I could.

Cranking Up the Heat

As grueling as the daily workouts were, the gym was the safest place for me at the ranch. When I was giving every last bit of energy and focus to running, lifting, spinning, or jumping, I didn't have time to be tormented by some of the gremlins starting to run loose in my head.

For the first few weeks, with so many of us and only one trainer for our team, I found I could easily fly under the radar, so I quickly fell into a routine. My mental endurance was another story. Early on, I could feel myself struggling to work through homesickness, vulnerability, and the loss of simple joys like texting a friend at lunch or just doing what I wanted to do on my own schedule. Each day took us higher on the learning curve and deeper into the workings of the Malibu ranch. Whatever control we thought we had went out the window, as we were at the mercy of the producers of reality TV. (Umm … U-N-C-O-M-F-O-R-T-A-B-L-E!)

Living all together in one house was interesting. Each team had its own room, but the common areas were open to all of us. I grew up living around a lot of people, so it didn't bother me to have so many strangers around on a regular basis. We didn't have to put a lot of thinking into our daily food choices—groceries were purchased twice a week, and we cooked our own meals. The kitchen was always a place of contention—who did or didn't do their dishes, who was messy, and who got stuck with all the cleanup—pretty much the typical "respecting others" adjustments you have to make when living in any community.

We began to establish our own routines, learning our way around the kitchen, where each team made its own meals. Mom and I aren't the world's greatest cooks, so we stuck with the basics like chicken and veggies and simple foods where it was hard to go wrong. She did most of the cooking, and I did most of the prep and cleanup. We had a system, and it worked fine, but we were pretty bummed when we realized that Bob's team had a real-life chef. In our minds, that equaled an advantage in the whole weight-loss game, and in our new world, even a percentage of a pound could make or break your time as a contestant.

On one hand, we lived by "expect the unexpected," always faced with twists and turns in the usual routine (including offsite trips and surprise exercises called "challenges" and "temptations"). On the other hand, we did have a basic daily regime:

7:00 a.m.	Wake up/shower/get ready for the day
8:00 a.m.	Prepare and eat breakfast in the dining area
8:30 a.m.	Low-impact cardio
10:00 a.m.	Finish cardio
10/10:30 a.m.	Grab snack and get changed
10:30 a.m.	Trainer arrives. Pep talk, start workouts
12:30 p.m.	Break for lunch
1:30 p.m.	Back to the gym for workouts
2:30 p.m.	Get pulled for an interview
3:30 p.m.	Return to gym, trainer leaves
4:00 p.m.	Snack
4:30 p.m.	Shower
5:30 p.m.	Start dinner prep
6:00 p.m.	Dinner
7:00 p.m.	Low-impact cardio
9:00 p.m.	Confessional on camera
9:30 p.m.	Get ready for bed

10:00 p.m.	Input BodyBugg food/exercise data and read
10:30 p.m.	Sleep
7:00 a.m.	Repeat

Right from the start, Mom and I kept things simple for our-selves—and we knew we'd have to stick together like glue and dig as deep as we could to survive. So we talked about this new world, its challenges and its joys, but mostly we talked to keep from losing our minds. We had new common ground, and we used this to begin to build a new relationship. We tried to keep the interactions with anyone we weren't sure of to a minimum. I did my best to keep short accounts with the other players, since I didn't want to find myself indebted to anyone or give anyone a reason to want to get rid of me when they had the chance.

The ranch facilities and gym were both open on a 24/7 basis to us. We had complete access to the gym for "homework"— training assignments we were given to do on our own time, in addition to any extra workout time we wanted to add ourselves. All around, the campus was pretty low maintenance, especially on the "dark" days, when the production staff was not on-site (we taped an average of four days a week). When the crew was there to tape, the schedule would become much more complicated. Often, they would want to tape something specific so we would have to be mic'd and ready to go where we were told to go and be there when we were told to be there. Going to the restroom required something equivalent to a hall pass since we couldn't just disappear during taping. Sometimes between camera setups we were put into a "TV time-out," meaning if the host announced something and the crew needed to move cameras, they would ask us to stay quiet and "hold that thought," so they could move and set up in another room without losing the momentum of a given scene or encounter. They wanted to capture the flow of a typical interaction and not miss any pieces of a conversation we were having while they were dealing with equipment and technical issues. Living at the speed of the camera crew seemed odd at first, but we got used to working at their pace, and after a while, it became second nature. It was much less hectic when the cameras were not around, but physically speaking, it was always exhausting. Our trainers came to work us out whether we were taping or not, but part of our workout was based on the honor system, since we did the homework portion on our own.

Having that structure was a lifesaver in many ways—we didn't have to think, just move to the next item on the list. It didn't leave us with much spare time, but we had just enough to start making and sharing observations about the other players. Several had already formed into cliques and alliances, and others kept to themselves as we moved forward.

By the end of the first week, everyone knew everyone else's story. The producer had told us up front, "Some of you know what story you are here to tell, while others of you will have to discover what we see in you." And so the production staff began digging deeper for the gold, looking for those priceless TV nuggets, which their instincts told them lay just beneath the surface in each team. At every interview, they would probe and ask questions and—like the crusty old prospectors panning in the stream—swirl it all around to see if anything shiny might appear.

The stress of trying to control the information flow—second guessing the questions and being overly guarded with my answers, all while trying to keep my escalating emotions in check—was getting to be more than I had bargained for. Added to that were the pressures of increasingly competitive game play and trying to act normal with my mother when I was feeling anything *but* normal. And of course, there was still the pressure from the game aspect of the show, which involved trying to get through the killer workouts and keep our numbers strong enough to last another week. I had started with a pretty simplistic picture of how it would go, and I hadn't realized how much more there was to this contest than simple weight loss. Call it being naive, but I totally underestimated the true intentions of some of the players. I was there to make amends with my mother and to get a new lease on life. I could not have cared less about being the last one standing at the end of it all. What I didn't want was a bunch of strangers trying to frame our story the way they wanted it to play out or telling me how to walk out the part with my mom. We would do fine left to figure it out on our own. Until we did, I wished everyone would turn off the bright interrogation lights and focus elsewhere. The stress was building on every front.

Each night, I was sick to my stomach with the fears of what the next day would hold. Mom would be fast asleep as I just curled up and stared at the wall. I had arrived at the ranch already loaded down with my own private emotional baggage, which I had not even started to unpack since I wasn't exactly in a place where I could process it all in a normal, healthy way. I did begin to let my mom know that things in my head were not good. I felt myself starting to shut down, and I went from struggling with insomnia to wanting to sleep whenever I could get away on a break—the telltale sign that things were truly out of control in my life: "Go to sleep and the pain goes away." I knew it wasn't about physical fatigue nearly as much as desperately seeking an escape from the increasing pressures.

Descent into Darkness

It wouldn't take long for the strain to start to show. It was only week two on the program when viewers got a glimpse of my internal battle and started to see the cracks in the dam that would quickly spread. Although my big breakdown would happen two weeks later, it wasn't written into the program's storyline until week five. Meanwhile, trouble was brewing. Not even to the quarter mark yet, I was already overwhelmed with the internal burden I was carrying. The surface conversations with my mom that were OK for a few days were now causing me more stress than expected. I wanted to get to the bottom of our common pain, but the prodding to do so by every producer was wearing both of us thin. This secret pain was gripping me so tight.... I was prisoner of my own internal torment.

Jillian was going over strategy with us in a morning meeting when it happened. The first piece of the dam broke off, and my tears began to flow. I did everything I could to hold them back—my greatest fear being Jillian's reaction, which could be anything from a simple, "Just suck it up, sister!" to her best Tom Hanks, "Are you CRYING? THERE'S NO CRYING ON *THE BIGGEST LOSER!*"

Instead, I was shocked when America's toughest trainer sent everyone else off to work out, then sat me down to get to the bottom of it all. Although part of me was terrified since I had no clue what to expect if I actually opened up to her, the bigger part was grateful to be able to release even a little of the steam that had been increasing every day in this pressure-cooker world. I began by acknowledging that part of the problem came from my feeling that I was the one responsible for holding everything together at home. There was no one else to do "mommy stuff" for Mia and IAM, like making meals, getting them to and from sports events and other school activities, and buying all the odds and ends needed by active, growing teens (most of Dad's money went to basic living expenses and keeping a roof over our heads). So beginning at eighteen and then again at twenty, I did what I believed to be the right thing by living at home instead of moving out to start my own life.

But despite having chosen to do this, I struggled with the pressure of getting everything right for them because I knew someone had to do it. It was more like a lovely dinner party I had been fully enjoying right up to the moment the last person left—and I suddenly realized I was the one stuck with the bill. My reaction the first time Mom moved out was shock and hurt, since that was my first indication we weren't the loving, happy family everyone thought we were. The pain of rejection and abandonment was unbearable. The second time she left, after we had all spent a year rebuilding together, the pain was too much and something broke inside me. This time, my hurt was accompanied by a deep sense of betrayal and an emotional withdrawal that would do far more damage than I could have guessed at the time.

Many people might view divorce as part of everyday life since the numbers tell us half of all marriages end that way, but to me, my parents' divorce might as well have been a death. I processed my pain very much like the death of a loved one because it *was* a deep loss in every sense of the word. I was brokenhearted that Mom wanted to leave what I thought was our happy home. Especially since doing so caused her to undermine the biblical principles my family had taught me. These were the pillars upon which I'd built my life. It shook me to the core and made me question my faith and understanding of what makes a believer different from anyone else. But what wounded me most about her decision that day was the overwhelming sense of personal rejection. She had calmly announced that she was almost packed and ready to go, that she would be taking both of my sisters with her, but not me. To an eighteen-year-old mind that made some sense because everyone knew I loved my dad. But to an eighteen-year-old *heart* there was nothing in the world that could have hurt worse than being abandoned and left standing on a curb as my mother pulled away without me to start her new life.

Jillian had the precision of a surgeon as she quietly felt around for the source of my pain, and I was overwhelmed by this kinder, gentler version normally hidden under her leather-and-chrome exterior. She asked some questions and acknowledged the difficult place I was in, while giving me her perspective. I admit I was a bit shocked as she told me she believed my mother's leaving was the best thing because Mom had finally put herself first in order to be happy.

"Michelle, have you ever put yourself first?" she asked me point-blank.

I shook my head no, and she went on to say that Mom's leaving could have been the greatest gift she had ever given me. It was hard enough to discuss it in the first place. But I also knew she didn't have all the facts, which was my fault since I tend to play everything in life close to the vest, only giving up information on a need-to-know basis. Jillian did share later that she hadn't known at the time that a lot of my hidden pain had to do with Mom leaving me personally, and my subsequent wrestling with issues of rejection and broken trust. But I couldn't voice my true heart yet, as it was all still a mixed-up bucket of unspoken pain and fear.

Although Jillian wanted to impress on me that I was worth putting myself first just as Mom had, it actually had the opposite effect. As practical as much of her advice was—particularly the part about establishing boundaries and not being a doormat— my struggle became that much harder because I fundamentally disagreed with her. My parents raised me to believe happiness came not by putting myself first, but rather by living by biblical standards and pursuing a calling that is much bigger than myself. It seemed that what Mom had done was at the expense of her own claim to live by scriptural principles. So while part of me was grateful for the encouragement and insights from my talk with Jillian, the other part was more confused than ever as I wrestled with the growing conflict within. The walls began to close in as I tried to make sense of it all, and I had no place to hide as I continued to break under the weight of the unresolved questions in my heart.

Beaten Black and Blue

After the first few weeks, the relationship dynamics between players started to get interesting. While everything remained amicable, various motivations and personalities surfaced once we had taken our road trip to the Grand Canyon in the third week and spent more time together. Little comments here and there gave hints about the way future loyalties would shake out.

Although the lines were drawn early, things didn't get too personal until week four when a major shift occurred in the group dynamics. As a prize for winning a "temptation" exercise, one contestant was given power to reassign each of the players from two-person teams to one of the two new teams—Blue (Bob) or Black (Jillian). The new Blue and Black teams would compete against each other until week eight. After that, the two teams would dissolve and each player would compete as an individual. The "temptation" that led to the team selections was a highly charged event as conflict broke out between the married couples, and a few individuals fought for control using tactics that took the game play into personal territory.

It was at this point Mom and I said good-bye to our pink T-shirts and hello to black.

Even though *TBL* is a weight-loss program, alliances are critical as a tool of survival. Strategy counts almost as much as weight-loss percentage since the votes of others can send either of the bottom two "losers" packing. With the yellow line marking off the two players losing the lowest weight percentage each week, the contestants fight to stay as far above the line as possible in order to stay on the ranch for one more chance at the $250,000.

Following the heated team-trainer reassignments, all bets were off, and an atmosphere of collusion and treachery set in for the remainder of the season. Any gray areas all but disappeared as the Blue Team tightened their strategy and became very vocal. They were strong, they were organized, and they were ready to crush the opposition in whatever way presented itself.

At first I was a bit intimidated by all the scheming, but then Mom and I just decided to stay as far away from the drama as we could, especially since we had our own unfolding issues. There were way too many land mines in this setup, and I knew I couldn't afford to be careless as we went forward. Furthermore, I couldn't understand how anyone even had time for all the extracurricular intrigue since it took just about everything we had in us to keep up with the physical requirements of the contest.

As for me, my focus was elsewhere. One of the most pivotal moments of my entire *TBL* experience—no, make that my entire life—lay just ahead.

Photo Album

Mom and me (less than a year old).

Me (3) feeding the ducks at the park. Probably one of my favorite pics.

Me (4), Drea (2), and Joseph (6) on a play day at the park in California.

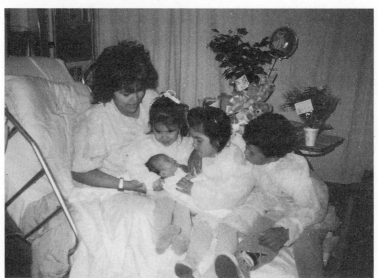

Mom, Drea (4), me (6), and Joseph (7) at the hospital meeting IAM for the first time.

Drea (5), Mom, and me (7).

My favorite pic of my dad and
me (8).

Me (8), Dad, Drea (6), and Joseph (9) on a Sunday morning in California before church.

Me (15) and Joseph (16). High school days!

Mia (6) and me (15) at church in Texas after an evening service.

Me (16), Nana (great-grandmother), and Joseph (17)
on the day Joseph and I graduated from high school.

Me (16), Mom, Joseph (17), Drea (14), Mia (6), and IAM (10) spending a day at home.

Drea (15), Mom, and me (17) in New York City for a concert.

Me (17), Drea (15), Mom, and Joseph (18) at a friend's house for a party.

Me (18), IAM (12), Joseph (19), Drea (16), and Mia (9). I organized this photo of all of us after my parents separated for the first time.

Dad, Drea (18), Mom, IAM (14), me (20), Joseph (21), and Mia (11). The last time we took a trip back to California together before my parents divorced.

Joseph (21), me (20), Amanda (sister-in-law), Drea (18), Dad, Mia (11), Mom, IAM (14). Last family Christmas photo in front of the house before the divorce.

Dad and Mom at Joseph's wedding. One of the last photos before they divorced.

Dad, Joseph (22), me (21), Drea (19), IAM (15), and Mia (12) at the Texas Motor Speedway for a race.

IAM (17), Drea (21), Joseph (24), Amanda, me (23), and Mia (13) together for a birthday party at home.

Mia (17) and me (26) at home for Christmas.

The "before" pic for *The Biggest Loser.*
Photo courtesy NBC Universal Photography

Mom and me. First day in the gym for *The Biggest Loser.*
Photo courtesy NBC Universal Photography

The "after" pic for *The Biggest Loser.*
Photo courtesy NBC Universal Photography

Me and Jillian at the finale. For me this picture shows the connection we had made as friends.
Photo courtesy NBC Universal Photography

Me and Micah. One of our first photos from after we started dating. We were watching a Christmas parade with my family in Fort Worth, Texas (2008).

Me and Micah. This was our first Christmas card photo we sent out to our families (2008).

Our wedding day (2009).

Micah and me on our honeymoon in Maui (2009).

I am Second taping in spring 2009. I hoped more than anything that my story would help others.
Photo by Trey Hill

I am Second taping in spring 2009. One of the hardest interviews I have ever done.
Photo by Trey Hill

I am Second taping in spring 2009. This interview stripped away all the "bling" of my life and allowed me to just speak from the heart.
Photo by Trey Hill

I am Second taping in spring 2009. The photo shoot after taping my interview.
Photo by Trey Hill

7

Losing My Life to Find It

Some of us think holding on makes us
strong; but sometimes it is letting go.
—Hermann Hesse

It was the water-tank "challenge" in week four that proved to be my perfect storm.

I remember going into it utterly exhausted, both mentally and physically, yet feeling an urgency to win because of the reward: letters from home. By this time I was dealing with raging homesickness and a need to feel comforted and supported by reconnecting with loved ones, if only through letters I knew had been sent and were waiting for me. I wanted so much to win this prize. The goal of the challenge was to stay balanced between two bars suspended on chains, one you held onto from above and the other you stood on while immersed up to your shoulders in water. This was not terribly difficult, as the water gave you buoyancy.

Until they started draining the tank.

Then it became a painful balancing act as you slowly began to support more and more of your body weight between the little trapeze-like bars above and below while the water emptied out. Before long, everyone began jerking and swaying and trying to stay perched on their bars, dripping wet in the cold night air.

Chink in the Armor, Chip in the Tooth

Before the challenge had even started, I realized that my foot bar was a little uneven. It was hard enough to stand there and keep my balance on a bar so thin and unstable, but the fact that it was also on a slant made it impossible. As the first few players wiped out, I knew I wasn't far behind them. One of my feet was squashed against the lower side chain and starting to go numb, so after a short while I gave in to the pain and had to drop out. Once eliminated, we were supposed to sit on our bars and await instructions to get down and swim out, generally timed with camera shots for a seamless exit. When they gave hurried signals for me to drop into the water, I tried to respond quickly but slipped down lower than planned because it was much deeper than I realized. I went underwater and panicked.

Because I had a helmet on, my first thought was that it might fill with water and pull me down, so I swam back up to the surface as fast as I could. Just as I reached the top, the bar that I had been sitting on (which had swung out when I jumped into the water) was returning back to its position, and *smack*—it hit me right in the face. There was a one-inch strip of the metal bar that had been exposed (the slant had caused the foam to scrunch down like the wrapper of a straw, leaving a part of the metal exposed). Of course, it had to be that one inch of bare metal that hit me square on my front tooth, chipping it. The impact made me start to cry immediately.

No! Not my teeth! Anything but my teeth! There it was. The last piece of armor that I relied on to keep me safe from prying eyes and judgmental thoughts—my smile—was stripped away, leaving me with nothing left to cover myself in this harsh and hostile place.

Tears poured down my face as I climbed up out of the tank. The athletic trainer saw what had happened and was waiting at the top to check on it. He examined my tooth and said comfortingly, "It's not too bad." Not too bad? What did *that* mean? It didn't matter—I was through. I cried for a while, then regained my composure and sat and waited with the other eliminated contestants. But in my mind, I had already turned the corner. I decided that this was the final straw.

Now, I realize there are worse things in life than a broken tooth. But let me tell you, when you've been ground down to nothing and you're trying to hold on to any semblance of dignity you can find, losing the one thing that had worked to hide your imperfections and protect you is no small matter. I was devastated, trying to hold it together as my carefully built defense system crashed down around me. And there I was, left vulnerable and exposed and with no desire to do anything but turn and run away.

Reopening the Mother Wound

That night, back in our cramped dorm room, I told my mom I was done. I announced that I was quitting the show and began gathering all my belongings and packing my bags. There wasn't much she could say to keep me there. My mind was made up, and there was no way anyone was going to talk me out of it. And history had proven she was never great at fighting to keep me. She didn't fight to keep me when she left Dad and took my sisters, and she didn't put up a fight when I told her I would have to love her from a distance, so I knew she wouldn't fight when I told her I wanted to leave our journey at *The Biggest Loser*.

My real fear was telling Jillian. On the one hand, I was afraid that I was going to disappoint her, and I knew what that would mean after the commitment we'd made to this journey. On the other hand, I was looking for confirmation that I was making the right choice, and part of me felt she would not waste any time by being concerned about me. When we first met in Grapevine, Texas, she had told me straight up, "Look, Michelle, I'm not here to be your friend," to which I had responded, "That's fine—I don't need any more friends."

What I hadn't planned for was the fear that would come with leaving Jillian and the deep connection I felt with her. We actually had become friends, and it made me sad to think about losing her in that way.

I had already played the scene out in my mind: I was certain that when I told her I couldn't go on, she would show me the door and never speak to me again. It was my "quit on her before she quits on me" defense that I had started to construct the day my mother (unknowingly) did the same thing by telling me she was leaving my dad. At that point I began believing that women are not to be trusted. Since I hadn't experienced anything to prepare me for the ripping that took place in my heart at the age of eighteen, I began to build walls around myself so that nothing like that would happen again. Apparently, I did a great job, because my relationships outside family and a handful of trusted friends became few and far between.

Although God had worked though various women to bring missing pieces into place, some of those women also hurt me. Two different managers had stepped into mother-like roles in different seasons and were precious and important parts of my life. And yet one of those relationships turned toxic, and I was brokenhearted as the abandonment scenario seemed to play out again. Why did women always have to leave me?

My mom, my supervisor, and situations with some of my coworkers reinforced my distrust of women enough to make me learn to keep my distance. Why trust them? They would only walk away as soon as things started to get a little tough. I didn't expect anything different from Jillian. Ironically, I was about to do what I accused all of them of doing—walk out because I couldn't handle the heat. But that didn't stop me. I had reached my limit, and I just wanted to run. As fast and as far as I could. For a split second I even thought, *Maybe this is what my mom felt like when she walked out of my family all those years ago.* What "tooth-chip moment" had happened to send her over the edge of her own ability to hold it together?

I decided I would have my mom tell Jillian because I was too scared to risk her reaction. That day on the ranch was a "dark" day, meaning there were no cameras on set, and Jillian was scheduled to arrive any minute. I was hiding out in the bathroom trying to get myself together because I didn't want the others to know what was about to happen.

When Jillian got there, my mom told her what was going on, and it wasn't too long before I heard a knock at the door. I hesitated for just a moment, then let her in, and was shocked to see that she wasn't angry at me.

"Hi, Peanut." (Jillian loves to give people pet names, and they usually change depending on the direction of the wind. Seriously.) "Renee told me you have decided to go home. And, Angel" (another pet name), "I cannot imagine what you must be going through, but what I can tell you is how brave you are for jumping on this journey with your mom. I came in here to tell you that, no matter what you decide, I will support your decision and love and respect your decision. But here is the deal: I want you to stay. And here is why: Babe, it's working. What you came here seeking, you are finding. For the first time in a long time you are in a space with no distractions, and you are being forced to face the very things you've been running from all these years. That's why you are scared. Please stay and fight through this, and I promise you it will be worth it."

Although I hadn't known Jillian for very long, she managed to gain my trust pretty quickly. That's what makes Jillian so great at what she does. Anyone can make people run on a treadmill or drop down and do push-ups until they puke, but it's a completely different thing to have the ability to get to the root of what's really behind all the weight. That is where Jillian really works her magic. Jillian had shown she heard me, and that meant the world to me, so I shared my heart with her.

In the midst of this crushing stress, my greatest immediate fear was a pretty superficial one: I was afraid of having no control of how all these emotions were going to come across on prime-time television. That scared me to death.

"Jill, I'm trying to be this good Christian girl, and all this is just so messy. Clearly, I'm broken. Who wants to see this?"

I went on to explain that my production-shaped brain was working against me in a big way on the ranch. As much as I tried to stay focused on the important issues, like making sure I was leaving for the right reasons and not bailing on myself or the relationship I was trying to rebuild with Mom, I kept getting hammered by my fears of appearing imperfect. I tried not to think about how all this would play out on the show, but my brain immediately went to *Will I come across as weak, messed up, or needy? Will viewers get bored with my continual breakdowns and decide to flip the switch from empathy to dismissal? Will America reject me in my weakest moment?*

Jillian's reaction amazed me, especially since I knew she made a living railing against weakness. But to my astonishment, she took the time to listen to me, extended grace and empathy to me, and gave the encouragement I needed to get me out of the bathroom and into the gym. Although I still stood firm in my decision to leave, she agreed to let me work out while I waited for the administrative details of my departure to be completed.

Standing at the Crossroads

As it turns out, quitting is harder than it looks.

It took days for the producers to figure out how to work it into the show. I felt as if they were dragging things out in hopes that I would just forget about quitting and decide to stay. Not a chance. Over the next week, I went through the emotional stress of telling my teammates and giving a three-hour exit interview to the executive producer while still working out and doing the challenges. They finally decided that at the next weigh-in I would have to give them my answer. This all took place over such a long period of time that it left me open to some ridicule from the other team. There was a moment in the "challenge" for that week when an opposing teammate brushed by me and said under her breath, "Just leave!"

And yes, I understood their scorn. No one had ever voluntarily walked away from *TBL* before. Thousands of people wanted to be here, wanted this opportunity. And here I was, ready to walk away because I was afraid of what people would think of me and my family. The day before the weigh-in, I still had the support of my mom and Jillian. But Jillian wasn't giving up easy. She had one last trick up her sleeve.

"Babe, again please hear me when I tell you, no matter what you decide, I will *always* love and adore you. Do you understand that?"

"Yes, Jillian, I understand, and you have no idea what that means to me."

And then Jillian handed me a phone.

"Babe, I want you to call your dad. I know how much you love and respect him, and I think you need to call him and tell him you are thinking about coming home and see if he has any words of encouragement for you."

Despite being somewhat scared at the thought of calling my dad and disappointing him, I gave in. And I'd love to tell you that during that call I found my voice and told my dad how certain I was that I was doing what was best for me—or even that I was able to simply describe what I was feeling and have a rational conversation about it. Nope. I cried and cried, and then I cried some more.

Jillian tried to help me get through it, and at one point she strongly encouraged me to address the issue of loyalty with my dad. Being a product of a divorced family herself, I believe Jillian personalized my pain and felt it equally as her own. She thought that perhaps one of my deepest issues was not feeling that I had the freedom to love Mom because of guilt and fear I would be betraying my dad. Although that figured into my struggle in a small way, it was so much more complicated than that.

Not having been able to process all the events of the past several weeks in any kind of safe, positive, and private way, I couldn't bear the idea of turning raw emotions during this phone call into sound bites to feed the hungry camera. There were things that my parents and I needed to work through together, but having everything played out in a glossy, packaged drama before America was not my idea of how anything meaningful or constructive could take place.

There were so many emotions churning inside me that night on the call, but nothing was sweeter than to hear the familiar voice of Dad. The same voice that had coached me through some of life's most difficult moments was on the phone helping to walk me through one of my greatest personal crises so far. I just cried and listened as my dad continued to encourage me, as always. "You can *do* this, Shelly.… Don't give up now.… We are all OK.… Do this for you.… Of course you can love your mom without losing me.… You need her.… You are an inspiration to your dad.… Don't you dare come home early—stay and work through this!"

Before hanging up, Dad looked for my answer on whether I would stay or go, but I couldn't assure him that I could find the strength to continue. I am sure he thought this call was no different from the many calls he had received throughout my childhood—I was always eager to go and stay with friends for overnight pajama parties, but come bedtime, I never failed to get homesick and always wanted to go home. And after every call, I could count on him coming to get me, no matter what time it was. But I was no longer a child, and this time I would have to choose for myself whether I would abandon ship or dig deeper than ever before to find what it would take to go on.

As the call ended and the crew shut down and left, Jillian told me one last time that she supported me and she believed that God wanted me here. I was actually a little stunned that she went to the God card. I was thinking, *Hey! You can't use God against me!* But she had crawled out onto the ledge with me, speaking truth that I wasn't yet ready to accept. She went even further than I could have hoped and told me that this was a safe place to fall apart, that she would be there for me to lean into as I processed this pain. She even promised not to judge me on the process I would choose to heal. "If you want to come to the gym wearing purple tights and a leopard leotard, I promise not to laugh."

Not long afterward, we both went our separate ways for the night.

Wrestling with God

As Mom drifted off to sleep, I was still wide awake and staring at the walls, trying desperately to turn my mind off and go to sleep.

And then it began. I started to cry softly, exhausted and frightened and finally feeling that I was getting to the end of myself. The full weight of the burden I had been carrying for years began to crush me, and I knew I couldn't hold it any longer. I had to let go, or I would go under with it.

I began to call out to God in my anguish, feeling like Jacob in Scripture as I wrestled it out in the night. *Why is it all happening like this? Why can't everyone just let me leave quietly? Why did they have to tell my dad? Why can't Jillian just let me go instead of fighting to keep me here? And why, oh why, can I not get some of Jillian's last words out of my head? Is there some truth to them that God wants me to see?*

"God, do *You* want me here?" As I said it out loud, the answer instantly resonated in my soul. I knew as I've never known anything that He did. *But why, God? Why this way, why now, why have You let this all happen?* I became more and more desperate as I cried out to Him. I was alone and overwhelmed—and suddenly right back in the moment when my mom left me, when I somehow thought the way back to "normal" was to push God away until I could fix everything myself and then show Him what a good job I had done. I realized how many years I had spent holding Him at arm's length, just as I did everyone around me. No wonder I had always felt as if I carried the weight of the world on my shoulders. I had insisted on holding on to everything that wasn't working in my world, in hopes that I could find a way to live up to the perfect image in my mind of who I wanted to be and who I thought my family should be.

And then it hit me—it hit me in the way only God can, with a gentle tapping on my heart. It was Proverbs 3:5–6.

It was one of my favorite passages from childhood, and it was the Scripture that I called on time and time again. But now I needed it more than ever. As my crying turned to sobbing, and then uncontrollable wailing, I knew what He was saying to me:

> *Michelle, lean not on your own understanding. In*
> all *your ways acknowledge Me, and I* will *make*
> *straight your path.*

I had been giving God the stiff arm, and He was patiently waiting, wanting me to give it *all* to Him: my hurt and pain, my parents, my family, my fears, my failures, my successes. I had been selling Him short all these years. I was saying all the right things, but I knew I wasn't living for Him.

I knew the old cliché, "Let go and let God." I had even written it in my own journal all those years ago, just days before my world officially imploded. But never before had it made such perfect sense—not until that night as I was lying there, crying into my pillow with a microphone under the nightstand and a camera mounted in the corner of the room. For the first time in my life, I let go of all my rigid perceptions, and I was shocked to find I truly didn't care what anyone thought of me—including me! That night, God found me broken, with a willing heart ready to give everything to Him.

It all hit me like a ton of bricks. God had my life in His hands. He had never left me. My crying out grew even clearer.

"God, I need You now more than I ever have. God, I want You to break my heart for what breaks Yours." And when my heart started to break, I got it. He showed me that my unforgiveness toward my mom was breaking His heart, and I knew that I couldn't run from this any longer. I knew I needed to deal with pain and not push it aside. I also knew I couldn't do it alone.

"God, help—help me to be a better daughter, sister, and example to others.… Show me how to love my mom like You love her, and help me never forget that I have already been forgiven of so much."

As I continued, I had to address the fact that I was currently on set with bags packed, ready to give up. God knew my heart was not there for a show or a grand prize. I was there to change from the inside out. So I professed to God that night, not in anger or out of obligation, but of my own free will, "God if You can use me, if You can use me in this situation, I'll stop fighting. I'll be present and accounted for. I'll do it all for Your glory, and I promise that when it is my time to go that I will go with a smile on my face."

I went on and on, rededicating my life to God for His work. "I know that I will be invincible until You say it is time to go. I don't have to worry about other people liking me or all the game play."

I was getting stronger with every word that flew out of my heart and mouth. "I will do this for You, but not in my own strength. I'll do it in Your strength, and I will give You all the glory in the end—no matter how this whole show plays out."

I was no longer questioning His path, but seeing that what He was asking for was my trust. He wanted me to trust that He knew the path and He saw the pain, but He also wanted me to lean on Him and not myself. I could hear myself boldly say, "God, You can use me—and if this show can help change people's lives—then I am ready and willing to do this. I'm all Yours."

The moment of truth came the next morning. Was last night real?

Yes. Despite waking up with a headache and puffy eyes almost sealed shut from crying so hard, I felt strangely and completely renewed. I sat up and looked over at Mom still sleeping, then glanced around our tiny room. I was astonished at how different everything looked. Last night I had never felt more lost and alone, yet in a matter of hours, I was in a totally different place. I had given it all to God, and the heavy weights of life (that for some reason I had spent years thinking were mine to carry) were lifted off me. I was a new creation that day.

In the light of this day, I saw my mom no longer as the source of my pain but rather as a person in need of love and forgiveness, just like me. Yes, I would still need God to help heal the gaping wound she had made so many years earlier, but for the first time, I was not looking to her or to myself to fill in the gap. I was now in God's capable hands and was free to love her without judging her.

That night at the weigh-in, I would have to account for my recent actions and give my final answer to Alison, our host, about whether I would stay and finish out the course. After we all entered the gym and took our places before the scale, Alison wasted no time as she quickly recapped my personal struggle and then asked me pointedly, "Michelle, what have you decided?"

For the first time since I had been at the ranch, I felt a strength and a peace resting on me that was beyond human explanation. Instead of cowering behind a defensive smile, this time I stood with a smile shining out from the inside—ready to give the answer that I could not give my father the night before. "Alison, I am going to stay. And whether I go home tonight, next week, or make it all the way to end, I am going to give it everything I've got. I am present one hundred percent." Last night had been a true game changer, and now this was a whole new experience.

I smiled with the knowledge that my heart toward my mom was changing too. Although there would be opportunities to continue the healing process beyond the ranch walls, I needed to focus on walking this out step-by-step and just surrender myself to what God was doing right then. I realized that forgiving my mom had less to do with her and her decision than it had to do with my trusting and being obedient to what God wanted of me. I was not being asked to offer her anything out of my own broken humanity, but to simply allow His love to flow through me, which could then begin the healing we both so desperately needed. With this new revelation, I had more than enough of His grace to show her love and patience, and to honor her. What He had given so selflessly and lavishly to me, I could now extend to her.

Looking back, I can see why it all had to happen the way that it did. I had wrestled with God and come out of it—like Jacob—with a new place to stand. Jacob's name was changed forever after his night at Peniel, and his new name, Israel, meant "one who contends and overcomes." That's what happened to me that night as God established me in a new place for the remainder of the contest—and even more importantly—for the rest of my life.

Not that I'm saying that things got easier after that. In many ways, they got even more grueling and intense the closer we moved to the final week at the ranch. The difference was that I was not the same girl. I had a new sense of purpose and resolve as I yielded to the process and allowed God to work in areas of my life I had never given Him access to before. No longer was this just a fitness program where I would walk away with new tools and techniques for my new body—it truly had begun to change me from the inside out.

When people ask about my relationship with God, I look back and see clearly that this was the true life-changing moment. I went from knowing about God to actually longing for a relationship with Him. Like Jacob, my life from that night on would be forever different. And just as Jacob walked from that time on with a limp that reminded him of his encounter with the living God, I accepted with a new and grateful heart my own "limp" as I placed my cherished childhood fantasy of the perfect life on the altar once and for all. As I humbly laid down my expectations and selfish demands of what life was supposed to look like for myself and others, I received a sense of freedom I had never dared believe could be mine. A feeling of wonder and awe filled me as my new eyes blinked open, and my imperfect but beautifully authentic life suddenly seemed like the perfect life for me. It was enough, and I was enough, and I was convinced that winning the lottery could not have made me feel a single atom richer than I did in that moment of release and acceptance.

Leap of Faith

As I said earlier, just because my commitment to the show's process had been renewed and my eyes opened to the new possibilities didn't mean that the demands of the ranch became any easier. We had made it halfway through the season, and I was feeling pretty raw after being pushed, pulled, berated, and challenged beyond anything I'd ever experienced before.

We were at the end of one particularly long day spent on what was called the ropes course. Each of the contestants was given a specific rope-and-heights challenge meant to expose any hidden fear of heights or claustrophobic tendencies and push us into new mental-endurance territory.

Mom and I had already completed our assigned challenges and had gone into relaxed-observer mode. Earlier, we had bravely climbed into harnesses for the ropes course and were hauled forty feet up to walk the catwalk from two different sides of an airborne log in order to meet in the middle. (Nothing symbolic going on there!) It had been a great success—meaning neither of us lost any limbs or had a panic attack midair. We finished our exercise and were brought back down in our getups of wire, hooks, and canvas. By this time, I was exhausted and thankful that we were done for the day. We cheered the other contestants on as they completed their own exercises. I was secretly relieved that Mom and I didn't have to perform the exercise known as the leap of faith, a particularly distasteful drill that required players to climb up to a small plank—a tiny strip of rough wood almost as narrow as a balance beam—attached to the top of an unstable telephone pole. The players would then stand up as they were swinging and swaying and proceed to leap off into the air as pulleys and ropes engaged to suspend them and keep them from falling headlong to the ground.

Just when everyone was winding down and the crew was planning to wrap for the evening, Jillian looked over at me with a grin and announced out of the blue that I was going to head up to the platform to take the "leap of faith."

I was stunned. Me? *Now?* I felt a rush of fear but also more than a little betrayal, as if Jillian had broken an unspoken pact between us because of the special bond we had developed. Her loud and gutsy style was so similar to Dad's that I felt more comfortable with her than many of the other contestants did, so I felt a closeness with her others did not. But this was too much. Mom and I had already done our challenge for the day, so why was she making me do this, too? Actually, I probably wouldn't have felt so frustrated if she wasn't asking me to do the one challenge I had dreaded since we had arrived at the course early that day. Even so, I knew that *no* was not an option.... You don't say no to Jillian. So

I took a deep breath and slowly climbed up the pole. When I got up there, I turned to the crowd below—and that's when I froze with a smile resembling the Cheshire cat's plastered on my face.

I had been here before.

Suddenly Jillian, the contestants, and the crew all faded away. There, instead, was my dad and a yard full of kids at a neighborhood pool party. I was eight, a bit small for my age, with dark curls and wearing my new ruffled swimsuit. I had been eyeing the huge spiral slide that the other kids were having such fun zooming down before hitting the water, screaming and laughing. I decided I wanted to try it too, so I got in line to climb up for my turn. But when I reached the top of the slide, I looked down—and suddenly changed my mind. It felt way too scary to be so high up, and I turned back, wanting to climb back down the ladder. But it wasn't that easy—there was a line of impatient kids pressing in behind me, and I began to panic, feeling trapped between them and the slide, which suddenly became the *last* place I wanted to be.

My dad's booming voice cut through the noise and fear. "Shelly! Slide down!" I scanned the pool frantically and saw him, smiling, as he waited with his arms held up toward me. He called again. "It's OK, Shelly. Just hold on and slide down—I'll catch you!" He seemed so far away!

"No, Dad—I don't want to! I want to climb back down!" I was shaking as I held tightly to the ladder, refusing to let go despite being trampled by kids piling up and over me onto the slide.

"You'll be fine! I'm right here!"

I peered over the top and shook my head at the twisting length of the slide.

I wasn't a great swimmer, but as my dad continued to encourage me and talk me through it, I finally decided to take the plunge. I braced myself, letting go of the bar and holding my nose, and slid down with a scream. To my amazement, I survived. I even enjoyed it!

Getting Unstuck

This time, it was Jillian's voice that broke through, calling my name and telling me to jump. Standing there in her fatigues, one sculpted arm was waving, the other on her hip. But she didn't know I'd morphed back into the frightened little girl perched at the top of a slide, wanting to come down but unable to. I was embarrassed by all the attention, and even the encouraging shouts and advice coming up from the people waiting for me to go through with this scary exercise only added to the pressure.

Then suddenly the script changed as Jillian, who was *not* my dad, was about to give up on me. "If you're not going to jump, then just climb back down!" she said, shaking her head. There was a hint of disgust in her voice.

No! My mind was spinning. I couldn't jump, but I knew to climb back down would be a defeat much bigger than I could deal with later. So after twenty-five agonizing minutes, I said a quiet prayer asking God to ease the fear in my head, and I finally decided to do it. I slowly got to my feet and inched forward as the wood platform swayed and wobbled. In a somewhat anticlimactic move, I half jumped, half fell off the platform. It didn't look like much, but still, I knew deep down that this was a defining moment in my life. Such moments don't have to be dramatic, they just have to be in the right direction!

After pats on the back and victory hugs from everyone, the night was finally over and people headed to the buses for the ride back to the ranch. Jillian stopped me as I turned to leave, her eyes piercing as she asked me the million-dollar question: "Michelle, why did you stay up there for a half hour? Why were you content to just sit there in your own fear with a smile on your face?" I looked at her with a faint smile and a shrug. After a moment of silence, we turned to go.

Those words kept ringing in my ears because they were all mixed up with past pain and future fears in a blurry picture I tried desperately to bring into focus.

Why *did* I just sit there for all that time?

I knew it wasn't the first time I had gotten stuck; it was just the most public. Which, of course, was at the heart of my fears—being "outed" that my life was not the perfect one I had always strived for but instead was flawed and filled with people (including myself) who made mistakes and hid them instead of addressing them honestly. I had been stuck in my fear for so much of my life that I had learned to accept my shutdowns as normal. Instead of reaching out and asking for help, over and over I would end up paralyzed by situations and events that left me with a sense of hopelessness. As I laid these things out before the Lord, I began to realize how much of my past had been spent crouching on platforms just like this, allowing my fears to immobilize me instead of choosing to jump.

I will never forget the rush of emotions and sense of release I felt as I recognized the power of what was taking place inside me. I am still humbled by the way God set it all up, and that He knew exactly what it would take to push me out of the little box I was living my life from. Rarely do we do these things alone. I needed the strength of others I respected—like my father, and then Jillian—to help the frightened little girl learn how to press forward instead of backing down or freezing in the midst of oppressive fear.

OK, so I may not have let out an inspiring banshee cry of "FREEDOM!" as William Wallace did in *Braveheart*. Maybe my brand of courage is more like a gentle statement by Mary Anne Radmacher: "Courage doesn't always roar. Sometimes courage is the quiet voice at the end of the day saying, 'I will try again tomorrow.'"[4]

8

Winning It

*He is my strength, my shield from every danger. I trusted
in him, and he helped me. Joy rises in my heart until
I burst out in songs of praise to him. The Lord protects
his people and gives victory to his anointed king.*

—Psalm 28:7–8 (TLB)

We had endured weeks of brutal gym workouts, humiliating let-
it-all-hang-out appointments at the massive scale, and the shock
of trading our familiar comfort foods for their stripped-down,
healthy counterparts. We had survived eight outdoor challenges,

where we got grass burns from skidding off the end of water slides, baked in 110-degree heat, and shook like jelly in our sneakers as we were hauled into the air in various contraptions and predicaments. We had roughed it at the Grand Canyon, where we camped with little running water and very little electricity, and survived tactical warfare among the contestants. We were the final five contestants, who had scratched and clawed our way to this point, and we were overdue for some news we could get excited about.

So when Alison passed out the tickets and announced we were heading to New York City for a three-day whirlwind makeover and TV taping, there was a collective shriek by the women at the table (and a pretty funny mock shriek by the last remaining male contestant, who knew better than to fight the estrogen dominance surrounding him).

Boy, were we ever ready to be dazzled by limos, stylists, Tyra Banks, Times Square, and (we would discover later) brief but oh-so-sweet reunions with loved ones we hadn't seen in almost two months. We still had several weeks to go before we would be at our final weight-loss goals, but we had shed enough that we felt ready to step out and show the world our tremendous progress. Most of us had dropped an average of fifty pounds in ten weeks— an astounding average of five pounds per week!

The City that Never Sleeps

It was a full-blown fantasy trip from start to finish, even if I was so exhausted that I fell asleep on the Ralph Lauren studio couch at

Macy's at 3:00 a.m. I had been waiting for my turn with designer Christian Siriano, and we had been warned by the producers that it would be a pretty intense pace and to catch any sleep wherever we could find it.

The highlight of the trip was an early "reveal" on *The Tyra Banks Show* in our sparkling, almost-finished bodies that had been made over from head to toe. We each made our appearance on the catwalk and got to chat with Tyra a moment before being surprised with a beloved family member who had been flown to New York for this special occasion. I was overjoyed to see my father come barreling out from backstage, grinning from ear to ear as he joined us to share this moment in the spotlight.

Afterward, we all took a walk through New York City and relished every bit of time strolling the streets and sidewalks with our family members. I'll always remember how strangely small this huge city suddenly seemed the moment we all looked up at one of the outdoor screens in Times Square. We let out a collective gasp as the faces of Jillian and Bob appeared out of nowhere—a surreal moment not unlike the wicked witch's appearance in the crystal ball in *The Wizard of Oz*—to crack the whip and remind us to exercise while we were up there in the midst of our pampering, socialite whirlwind. But even their big-screen scolding couldn't dampen our enthusiasm for those glorious three days we escaped the harsh and unpredictable world of *TBL* boot camp.

Once we finished that evening, the contestants pretty much split up and did their own thing for the rest of our trip. Mom and I had been waiting the whole show for a fabulous trip and a makeover, but now having family there changed everything. Instead of hanging out together, we each had our own families, so it made for a completely different experience. Things had been a bit awkward from the start since I had never met my mom's new husband, but I wouldn't learn anything more about him by the end of the trip. From the initial van ride, where my mom took her seat with her husband in the front and Dad and I sat in the back, to the last day when we were all packed up and put on planes headed back to the ranch, the space between us felt like magnetic fields repelling each other.

At one point, the producers asked the four of us to sit down together for a meeting and a chance to talk about our feelings. But there was no way that I would take such a delicate situation and have it made public when real people were involved. Not only would it have been cliché, I also didn't want to put either of my parents on the spot like that. The timing felt all wrong. Luckily, the idea was dropped.

Fortunately, there was so much going on with a group our size that we were able to avoid a lot of otherwise awkward moments. Getting to know everyone else's family helped balance (or cover) the strangeness of my family dynamic. Either way, the entire group seemed to get along well, and nothing could ruin our adventure. We were in New York!

We spent the rest of our brief stay sharing a little bit of the *TBL* experience with our family members as we dragged them off to gyms and pulled them into whatever workouts we could improvise while there. Mom headed for the Brooklyn Bridge with her husband while Dad and I jogged and enjoyed the rest of our time together.

I had no idea how much had taken place in the time I had been gone. First, my father broke the news to me about his engagement to Tracy, a woman I hadn't even met yet (he had begun dating her right after I left for California). I remember being all over the map with this news. There was a huge part of me that was so happy for my dad that he had been able to connect and find true love again. In that moment, I could see the happiness oozing out of him, and it made me feel comfortable and happy in return. Then he hinted that my brother and his wife had some exciting news to share with me, but wouldn't tell me what. Talk about feeling out of the loop! My brother Joseph and I were the oldest two Aguilar children and shared a special bond, so hearing he had news made me miss him so much. (I would learn later they were expecting their second child!) Finally, Dad shared the difficult news that my former supervisor (my "adopted" mom from the network) had decided to go ahead with her divorce. My head was spinning—all this happened in the three short months I had been away? It was a roller coaster of emotions, and it was as if at every turn I was getting new information about the life I left behind. Yes, part of me was about to stick my fingers in my ears and shout, "La, la, la! Not listening to you!" to block his words. I wanted to know everyone was doing well, but so much big news was a complete shock.

It was a real wake-up call for me. When I realized how quickly things change, I knew that I needed to come back home changed as well. My drive to finish strong was fueled by knowing life was moving at a rapid pace, and I no longer wanted to sit on the sidelines. And furthermore, the pressure was on to not go home the following week, because now I wanted to show them all that I could make it to the end.

Alas, before we knew it, our fairy-tale trip to New York was over, and Mom and I were back at the ranch in the gym with Jillian (who was none too pleased with our girly-girl primping and the lost gym time we would now have to make up before that week's weigh-in). As much as I had enjoyed the trip, I could see why Jillian hated the distractions outside the gym since spending time with my dad in New York—even though it was time well spent as we exercised together—stirred up my homesickness in a big way and caused me to realize how terribly I missed my family and friends. Not to mention that stress works to sabotage any serious weight-loss goals. While Jillian and I might have been worried about what the New York trip would look like in terms of the numbers on the scale at the next weigh-in, we simply had no time to sit and worry. We had work to do.

Finding My Voice

Although my night of wrestling with God set the tone for the rest of my stay and was the single most significant event of my *TBL* experience (as well as my life), there were a handful of other defining moments at the ranch that helped me move forward in my understanding of who I was and who I wanted to become. Although my "leap of faith" victory is one that I will always treasure, there was another, even more powerful, experience that is forever etched in my heart as a truly life-shaping moment when I stepped out into a new place, never to go back.

You could say it was when I finally found my voice.

Language of Tears

As someone once wrote, "Tears are words the heart can't express."

Say what you want about crying, tears are their own language—and it's a language that I have been quite fluent in over the years. I'm not completely sure why I have always cried so easily, or why I have been so shy, but there are a few suspects. To start with, my family has an interesting blend of Native American, Italian, and Mexican ethnicity, and although my grandparents on both sides spoke Spanish, neither of my parents passed that part of our heritage on to us, and I had to learn how to speak Spanish in high school just like everybody else. With all the questions I would get about my culture mash-up, I would sometimes teasingly describe myself (with all the various influences) as a bit like a coconut— "brown on the outside and white on the inside." Early on, we did have a lot of exposure to the Hispanic culture in California, which is one where women aren't necessarily encouraged to be assertive or strong in a visible way.

Even my relationship with my dad was a double-edged sword in terms of my own development. Although I was enormously blessed to feel the security of having a doting and loving dad around, his powerful personality cast a huge shadow on the lives of us kids, which encouraged submission and shaped my personality in ways that neither of us probably realized at the time. Growing up, I never needed to fight my own battles because I knew he was always behind me, and all it took was for me to cry out to him and he would be right there to fix whatever was wrong. Whether it was coming to get me in grade school after a particularly tear-filled morning, or picking me up from a slumber party after midnight when I realized I was scared and wanted to go home, or showing up when, as a teen, I phoned to tell him about a bully (whose white-as-a-sheet face when Dad drove up confirmed that guy had picked the wrong girl to harass)—I had the best and most supportive dad any girl could ask for.

But perhaps in the long run, what I always thought was a blessing played into my shyness and struggle with feeling helpless. I never had to stick up for myself or really even fully trust God because my earthly dad was always there to figure things out for me.

But I was an adult now, and finally poised for a jailbreak out of a world where I expected others to interpret my tears and figure out what it was that I needed when I cried. I was ready to learn, once and for all, how to stand up and speak my piece when necessary in a calm, clear, and commanding way.

Shedding Tears and Fears

Even before I stepped up on the scale for the finale win that would launch me into my new life, I had already won some of my greatest personal battles, and the $250,000 was really more of a celebration of what I had won rather than the prize itself. As wonderful and useful as money is in life, we all know it is a finite resource, and—unless you are privileged to be born into it or have lottery payouts or royalties or dividends to support you for the rest of your life—at some point the money will run out, and usually quicker than you think it will.

Which is why I am far more grateful for the intangible, life-changing gifts I received from *TBL* that have no expiration date (or taxes, for that matter).

At the ranch, so much had taken place as I walked out my own personal journey, yet it wasn't until we reached the ninth week of the show—'80s week—that I had the profound and defining moment concerning my ability to find my voice and vocalize my needs and expectations. Although the incident that brought it all to a head made its way on to the program, there was a far bigger story going on.

In this segment of the show, Jillian was doing interval training with me on the treadmill, and stated for the camera, "Lately, Michelle cries every time she gets on the treadmill—I don't know why she cries!" The viewers see Jillian doing her typical job of pushing me to get me through the workout, screaming at me to never say that I can't do something. And that in itself is not the problem, since one of her strengths is the ability to pull people out of their perceived limitations.

But this time, it wasn't about her tough-love approach that we were all used to as she would regularly yell at us during our daily gym routines. It was about me learning how and when to speak up—not just for that moment, but for my future.

What started it all was when Jillian went off on me *after* I had gone out of my way to meet her exacting standards. During my final countdown on the treadmill, I had jumped ship three seconds too early—before it had come to a complete stop—instead of waiting and stepping to the side on the final count of one. This is a no-no with Jillian. She was totally ticked off at me because I was exhausted and couldn't hang in there. I kept crying and saying, "I can't … I can't … I can't do it!" (another trigger for Jillian). She yelled at me, "You need to push through!" That part was no big deal and pretty typical of a lot of our workouts. At this point in the game, her yelling didn't faze me.

So after she nailed me for my sloppy finish, I knew I was wrong and got back on to complete it correctly. I did it exactly the way she demanded. Then, after I finished doing what she told me to do, exactly the way she told me to do it, Jillian went off on me: "Don't you EVER tell me you can't do something—don't you EVER say you can't. If you don't want to do it, just say, 'I don't want to do it.' But don't tell me you can't!"

I was surprised and got angry at her, thinking, *That's too much! I mean, why did she scream at me when I did everything she wanted me to?* In typical passive style, I held it all in, gritting my teeth and staring at Jillian while she was on her rant. But as soon as she was finished, I burst into tears and walked away, heading for the stoop outside the gym, where I cried out of exhaustion and at her unfairness. My typical response to injustices (both big and small) has been to expect whoever hurt me to realize their mistake and do what they should to make it right. *Surely she'll understand what she did and that this was traumatic for me and that she shouldn't have yelled at me.* I got myself together and went back in after my crying spell with my pitiful little swollen face and red nose, figuring she would see that she hurt me and apologize. Tears have always been my way of saying, "That was too much.... Back off.... I'm hurt—so don't be mean to me anymore."

Instead, I was stunned when Jillian saw it as an opportunity to dig in more. She started in on me as soon as I got back, announcing sarcastically, "Oh, Michelle, did someone hit you in the face? You look like you've been beat up! Why are your eyes so puffy?"

Chasing Down My Freedom

I was beyond upset. I had expected at least a little sympathy and thought, *What's the matter with you, Jillian? You're not getting it— this is my expression of sadness! You're supposed to see my tears and realize you were wrong and say you're sorry. Why aren't you being nice to me?*

But I bit my lip and didn't say anything, and it wasn't long before we were finished for the day. Jillian said her good-byes and walked off, and suddenly the old fears of abandonment and rejection kicked in when I saw her leaving without having acknowledged my tears and pain. *I'm crying and upset, and she doesn't care!* I felt a sudden rush of emotions exploding inside. First, I needed her to understand what she did and why it caused me to react the way I did, and at the same time, I was afraid I might lose her like every other important woman so far in my life if I didn't set things right, so I took off to catch her. She turned to see me running up behind her and laughed, saying, "What? Are you coming back for more? What do you want?"

My heart was pounding in my chest, and I summoned every ounce of courage inside me as I went toe-to-toe with her. "I need you to stop yelling at me, Jill. I really can't take it anymore, and if you keep yelling at me, well … I won't work out with you anymore."

Jillian stopped, and a surprised half grin grew on her face as she listened to me blurt out my charges and demands. "It's just too much. You yelled at me even after I did what you asked me to do. So I guess it doesn't matter if I do it right or wrong— you're going to yell either way! But I did the right thing, and you shouldn't have yelled at me. I'm serious—I won't work out with you anymore if you yell at me like that again."

I was shaking like a leaf as I stood there and delivered my ultimatum. So this was what "Feel the fear. Do it anyway!" was all about! But it was Jillian herself who had taught me I needed to draw a line—and I was starting with her. The amazing thing is that up to that point, I had not been strong enough to stop her when she went into steamroller mode.

But she got it. She shrugged as she calmly replied, "You're right, Michelle. I went too far, and I won't do it again. I'm sorry."

I stood there in stunned silence. On the one hand, I was completely unprepared for Jillian's concession. On the other, I wasn't totally sure if there would be an unseen price to pay for my moment of courage. I wondered if maybe there was a catch—if she would punish me the next day by making an example of me, or picking on me, or beating on me, or ignoring me. I was used to her yelling—her normal volume level during workouts is "yell" —but you always knew when Jillian had a burr under her saddle about any of us, and we could expect some level of punishment in the gym until she worked us enough to get over it.

But it was nothing like that. The next day, it was as if we were on a clean slate and moving forward with a new respect on all levels. I was dumbfounded that it was that simple. Just as wandering Dorothy and her friends discovered in *The Wizard of Oz*, I learned that there was nothing I needed that I didn't already have. I just had to have enough pressure placed on me to bring it out.

This incident was a deeply impacting one for me—after years of sitting passively in my pain, expecting others to interpret my language of tears and respond to my cries, I had finally found my voice. My revelation was a bombshell. I finally got it that crying meant nothing to Jillian. She hadn't responded at all to my tears, yet she immediately responded to my clear and specific vocalizing of what I needed and expected. It was like living in a foreign country when finally the day comes when you've learned to speak the native tongue. Suddenly, all these new doors are open to you, and you can begin to participate in life on a far deeper level than before. She taught me a lot about making others respect my boundaries, and she demonstrated it by honoring my request for fairness once I stood my ground with her. It was a moment of sweet victory as I realized the untapped power I had carried all along and the implications for how I would develop my new communication skills once I got back home.

Fully Authentic

Interestingly, up to that point, part of my relationship with Jillian was not completely genuine—I had been walking on eggshells as I tried to appease and placate her to keep the infamous pit bull in her contained. I think I spent so much time and effort trying to stay clear of her triggers that I wasn't really getting the full benefits of her coaching. Fear shuts down the ability to receive, and by confronting my fears, I had begun the process of reopening spaces in my heart that I didn't realize had been blocked for so many years.

Our relationship changed that day. Not only was I able to be more honest with Jillian, and therefore more effective in my dealings with her, but I could feel God doing a deep healing in my heart in regard to the breaches of trust I had suffered with all women. I saw that part of my pain came from my inability to identify and take ownership of my needs in interactions and relationships—to speak up and set guidelines. Instead, I was expecting others to read my mind and treat me with the fairness and respect I felt they should see I deserved. Acknowledging my own contributions to these broken relationships was a painful but important step in reclaiming territory lost to the enemy. I would begin that day to dismantle—piece by piece—my cage of learned helplessness that kept me from voicing my needs and expectations in a healthy, productive, and adult way.

On My Own

We were now almost to the twelfth and final weigh-in before heading home for the three months leading up to the finale. Mom and I were the only original pair to make it all the way to the finals together (the husband of another contestant had been sent home and later returned to the ranch) and with all the focus on our relationship schism, it would be easy to overlook Mom's great accomplishment as a player in the contest. I don't think what the viewing audiences saw at home did my mom justice, so I want to emphasize what an amazing feat getting that far was for Mom, who had both weight and age to overcome. She proved herself a worthy athlete and competitor on many fronts (just ask me—I had to bribe her with a designer handbag so she would let me win one of the challenges that she would have walked away with otherwise) and lasted much longer than many other younger, stronger contestants.

Her formidable ability to win at the mental aspects of the various challenges emerged early on, but it was during week six on the circular balance beam challenge (where the contestants had to balance while walking the circumference of a pool as many times as possible) that she was able to shine for the Black Team as the one player to complete the full twenty-five laps—nine of those as the only player left! She was a great partner in this adventure, and aside from the personal rebuilding we were able to begin, we talked through many of the more difficult aspects of the program together like teammates.

So at the eleventh hour, the week before the final weigh-in, it was difficult to see Mom have to pack and leave after slipping below the yellow line and being voted off by the other remaining players. Because we were the last two Black Team members, she did not have enough votes to keep her on the ranch. I was disappointed about her loss of her own chance to win, as well as her leaving me as the last Black Team member standing. (Being alone, you may have guessed by now, is one of my least favorite things.) With the last three Blue Team members gunning for me, I knew finishing the season on top wouldn't be easy. At the same time, it seemed fitting that I would take the final lap by myself as I stepped up to a new place above the fears that had always had the last word in my life. Just as little David chose his five stones for his showdown with the giant Goliath in Scripture, I knew I would need to focus as never before to knock down the walls of fear and emerge with the top numbers that final week.

That night after the elimination vote, I went back to my empty room, while down the hall, the Blue Team celebrated their perfectly coordinated victory and vowed to be the last ones standing as we went to the final weigh-in. They were looking for an all-Blue finale to secure Bob his first Blue Team grand prize winner, and with only one Black Team member left their odds looked pretty good.

But that only made me more determined to go all the way.

My "Safe Word"

Jillian came to me the final week of the contest with a serious look on her face.

"Michelle, we have to turn it up a notch. I know that freaks you out, and I know that scares you, but we have to go for broke here. Now, I need to know up front that you are getting on this ride with me. I will do everything I can for you. I will be here for you, and will do everything humanly possible to help you, but I need you to show up. I need your A-game. I'm telling you, I need the absolute drop-dead best you can give me this final week."

I had never seen Jillian so quietly intense, and a wave of fear came over me as I wondered what that would entail. I paused a moment, then looked at her and said softly, "OK, I'll get on this ride with you. But just one thing first—can I have a safe word?"

She responded, "What?"

"Can I have a word that, in case everything gets too much and I don't know how to tell you, if I just yell this word out, you'll stop hammering me?"

Jillian chuckled and replied, "Well, yeah, I guess. Geez, no one's ever asked me for a safe word before. What do you want it to be?"

I said, "How about *Ferrari?*"

So that was the deal. She knew that at any point during the week, during any workout, if I yelled "Ferrari" and walked away, it was too much—and she wouldn't argue with it because it was my honest limit. Before that time, I was always terrified I might hit the wall at any given time but wouldn't be able to vocalize it. I thought that if I could have one word—just one word—to express when I was hitting the wall, then I could relax a little and focus on the task at hand.

The funny thing was I never used it. I think simply knowing that I had an emergency button just in case I did need it was enough—and took away some of the fear of not being able to speak up for myself if the time came when I really needed her to back off.

Jillian went to the wall with me, staying right alongside me all night in the gym (11:30 p.m. to 4:30 a.m.) the last night we worked out, to the chagrin of everyone on the Blue Team. They had already lodged complaints that it was not fair because they had to split Bob's time among themselves whereas I had all of Jillian's. Of course, I'm not sure exactly when they figured out that if you send all my teammates home, then yes, I'm going to get Jillian's attention all to myself.

After five hours of "last-chance" intensity workout, I had given everything I had and then some. With sweat dripping off me and every muscle twitching, I finally looked at Jillian and said, "I'm done. I can't do any more."

She just nodded her head and responded, "OK. Go lie down for twenty minutes, then get up to weigh in at five thirty."

That was it. I never had to use my safe word—I just looked at her after I had given my all and said, "I'm finished."

As we walked away together, she looked at me and said, "All right. We've done everything humanly possible. We give it to God now."

Winning Going Away

The final weigh-in on the ranch at week twelve was surprising in more ways than one.

As the last Black Team player standing—representing all the others who had fought under the same banner—I felt an intense rush of pride and hope as I stepped up to the scale for the very last time on the ranch. Jillian gave me a slight nod of support as we both stood waiting, our eyes burning holes in the board to see if her blood-and-guts training methods had been enough to send me to the finale. As the numbers flipped to reveal a nine-pound/5.35 percent weight loss, the biggest of the evening, my heart soared. I leaped off the scale and ran down the steps to meet Jillian, where we hugged and laughed in a dizzying moment of triumph.

It had been enough.

I ended the on-campus season at 162, a substantial 80 pounds less than the 242 I'd started with just twelve weeks before. The nine pounds were a shock since I had just dropped ten pounds two weeks prior, which had been my biggest number for the entire show except for the first week's loss of seventeen pounds. (The first week is in its own category since just about everyone dropped an insane amount of weight between all the water weight and the fact that our bodies hadn't had time to figure out what was going on and start to conserve energy or get messed with by hormones.)

The other big surprise was that Alison announced that the husband-and-wife team—who had both fallen below the yellow line and were up for elimination—would not have the same ability this time around to choose who would be eliminated and who would go on. In the final twist of the program, she announced that this time it would be America who would vote to decide which of them would go on to compete in the finale. They were each to offer their best pitch to the viewers, who would then vote. The results would be revealed the night we all returned to Los Angeles for the finale, our final shot at the $250,000 grand prize.

When the husband and wife later explained that they both told the viewers to vote for the wife—because that was the sacrifice this loving husband made so his wife would have a shot at winning—I knew they had made a fatal error in judgment. They may have been able to dominate the other contestants, but even I knew that America doesn't like to be told what to do.

Following the weigh-in, where one member of the Blue Team and I became the two confirmed finalists, each of us was taken individually back to the gym for a final look at how far we had come. Earlier, we had viewed footage of our time at the ranch and the journey we had completed. Since we had been pouring out everything we had without a lot of tangible feedback up to that point, this exercise was like holding a life mirror up for us to see the dramatic changes that had happened so far. Combined with a trip with Jillian back to the original hill I had conquered at the beginning of our journey, it was encouraging and inspirational, and I tucked the images away deep in my heart.

It had been some time around week six when Jillian told us that at the end of the course they would compare our new, sleeker bodies with our original selves by standing us next to our life-size "before" images. She said something at that time that—looking back with new eyes—was pretty profound: She asked us to be kind to our former image. That instead of being disgusted or ashamed, we should look at who we were only weeks before and be proud of what that person had chosen to do to bring us to this place. At first, I did not understand the importance of the exercise and didn't like the idea of having to face so much of me. I wondered how I would respond to the old, unhappy me.

Standing in the gym with Jillian that night, when the light flipped on, I stood face-to-face with my extra eighty pounds. When I saw the life-size "pre-*TBL* Michelle" for the first time, I was surprised by my reaction. I didn't feel any sense of loathing or even embarrassment. Instead, I realized I felt grateful for her and proud of who and what she wanted to be. (I often refer to my old self in the third person.) I am certain that my "before" photo will follow me around for most of my life; that's just the way it is. But I look at her and can honestly say I know what she is capable of. She was strong enough to get me here and to hand off the baton to her future-self teammate. Now, who knows what the new Michelle will do with this new body and new mind-set, but one thing is for sure—if the old me could do it, then I'm sure the new me can too.

So when I see her around (I never know where she'll pop up since I have years of her stashed in various family albums and friends' wallets and photo frames), I smile and say "hi," and let her know not to worry, because I am doing just fine.

Home Stretch

Once I got back to Fort Worth and began the final three-month preparation for the finale and big reveal of the next *Biggest Loser*, I was determined to put everything I had learned at the ranch to work in this fight of (and for) my life. Although we still had the team dynamic going with weekly conference calls—in which the entire cast was to report in to the production department so they could keep tabs on our progress—I rarely participated. It was a purely strategic decision on my part, since early on in the calls I felt like the odd man out and knew I would do better if I disengaged and did it on my own. Having the cast on the call each week took me back to the ranch with all its drama and distracting personalities. I needed to focus, and I always did better when things were quiet and all the white noise dropped to a minimum.

So I sent in my weekly data by email, and Jillian and I set up our own communication schedule. She was always available for questions and to offer any help I needed as I transferred my workout routine into the real world. Even with the support I received, it was still a bit of a jolt to lose the full-time training and nutritional guidance I had grown used to. But I was hopeful that I had returned home with enough motivation and knowledge to carry me through the next three months.

My Motivation at Home

Before *The Biggest Loser*, I had small dreams, but I had always wanted a story—a powerful testimony to share with others.

Growing up, I would hear about amazing transformations or people whose lives had been saved. They were delivered from addiction to drugs, set free from gang life, and given strength to overcome abusive pasts—all had received grace from God and had changed their lives dramatically. But that wasn't me. I was just a little girl who grew up a Christian. I had lived a "good" life from a young age, and I knew right from wrong. I thought my story would never be good enough to share with others. But a very small seed fell into my heart each time I heard the testimonies of other people. I said small prayers that maybe one day something interesting would happen to me and I would have something to share. But until then I would be quiet. Very, very quiet. Now here I was, a finalist for *The Biggest Loser* with the chance to win it all, and I finally had a platform from which I could share my story—and be used by God to make a difference in the lives of others.

The last part of my *Biggest Loser* journey, the part between leaving campus and coming back to Fort Worth to prepare for the finale was the most challenging for me physically, but it had an end date.

I've always thought that what matters most is the character you display when no one is looking. During those months, people hadn't yet started to recognize me from TV, so for the most part no one was watching. At the gym for those three months I was home I had anonymity—but every decision I made regarding what I put in my mouth and how much I exercised would be on display on December 16, 2008—the day of the finale. There were good days, when I was excited about getting up and facing the tasks ahead, glad to be one day closer to the end of this physical hell on earth. But there were bad days too. I was tired of all the workout schedules, tired of living a life no one could relate to, and sad that I felt trapped in the gym. But all these days combined to get me to the finale. It was not one decision, one bad day or one good day that would define me. It was all of them mixed together.

Still, one day jumps out clearly in my mind when I think of those final months leading up to the finale. It started out well, but after about three hours of cardio I was mentally done. The next thing I knew, I began to cry. I was walking on the treadmill and could feel the stares of the other gym patrons, but it wasn't enough to stop me from crying. I felt drained at that moment. I was trapped, and I wrestled with questions: *Why am I doing this? And for whom?* The lines blurred. This day was becoming a really bad day.

I lost my drive to keep going, and pushing myself was out of the question, so I stopped and got off the treadmill and walked out of the gym. I got into my car and bawled my eyes out. I wanted to quit. I spent about twenty minutes in the car unsure of what to do. But then I remembered my conversation with God that night back on the ranch. I decided to go back in and try one more time to finish my day strong. I knew I needed to trust God: that He could physically get me through and that I could turn this thought process into a healthy one. I went back inside, scrolled through my music playlist, and found "Desert Song" by Hillsong. I got on the elliptical and played this song. I began to cry once more—but now it was because I heard the words of the song and

I knew that God was still able to get to me in this season of my life. He heard me. He was faithful to supply what I needed. He could be my strength. He would provide exactly what I needed to not give up.

That day counted, and God got me through to the other side of my pain. I didn't quit that day or any day after. That experience supplied all the fuel I needed to finish strong and make it to the finale, knowing I had given it my all.

Surrendering to Success

I knew God was up to something from the moment I woke up after my nighttime epiphany back in week five. There was a new sense of hope and strength that morning that was not there before, and it allowed me to settle into a powerful, steady rhythm that was exactly what I needed to finish the journey I had begun several months before.

When I returned to LA a week before the reunion extravaganza that would end with the announcement of season six's *Biggest Loser,* I was filled with excitement and a sense of heightened anticipation. We had to fly in early for medical and health tests, wardrobe fittings, a photo shoot for our "after" shots and an individual walk-through to familiarize us with the set. I had been completely sequestered for the week leading up to, and including, the day of the finale. Although the at-home players (those who had been voted off during the season but who were competing for the at-home prize of $100,000) all stayed in the same hotel and could be together, the finalists were not permitted to see one another, and the show's staff went so far as to place each of us in different hotels. Because I had disengaged weeks earlier by opting out of the conference calls, I had no idea who was struggling and who was going to be coming on strong at the finish, but it worked better for me that way by keeping the pressure and anxiety to a minimum. I had lost another 30 pounds beyond the 80 I had lost on the ranch for a total loss of 110 pounds, which translated to 45.45 percent—almost half—of my former self.

The live two-hour program built up momentum as all the at-home contestants came back to compete for the $100,000 prize and share the inspiring results of their continued transformations in the real world. It was difficult not being able to see any of them as I waited patiently backstage in my own green room that was sandwiched between the other two finalists'. I tried to get info from the different staff people coming in and out—*What did they look like? Were they amazingly fit?* No one would give up the goods.

I had an endless line of people stopping in to wish me well prior to the show's opening, but once it started, that was it. I was alone with my thoughts, without even a TV to watch all the excitement I knew was going on around me. I had to guess who American had chosen to compete as the third finalist.

It was a total information and sensory blackout right up until the final minutes of the show. When it was my turn to punch through a life-size poster of my old self to join everyone on stage, it was truly a spectacular moment for me. And a moment was all it was—they then quickly whisked me backstage again to change into my weigh-in clothes so I could return to decide the order of the finalist weigh-ins—a privilege I earned as having the top weight loss that final week on the ranch. I chose myself to be last, hoping it would be the "best for last" moment that I was praying for. Fortunately, there was a commercial break right before my turn at the scale. It was just enough time to give some hugs to the other contestants and to gaze around the packed-out auditorium and capture this once-in-a-lifetime moment that would be mine forever.

It was a bit surreal to see the new, healthy versions of all my cast mates and *TBL* family. The women looked dazzling in slinky sheaths and cocktail dresses and the men looked sleeker than I'd ever seen them, wearing everything from denim to suits. After so many years of drowning in shame and self-rejection, it was a night we would all remember as everyone's fifteen minutes of fame came together in a joyful celebration of life and all its potential. We were all shining stars that evening, basking in the love of family, friends, and millions of at-home "extended family" as we displayed the fruits of our labors and lived out the dream so many of the viewers had dreamed right along with us.

I was thrilled to see so many of my own family members all sitting together, and I scanned the clamoring crowd, wanting to memorize every face and the signs and banners waving in support. My favorite was the "Michelle is the New Black!" sign that made me smile as I looked down at the black T-shirt I had worn to the end in a show of solidarity and triumph. When it was my turn to weigh in, Alison announced that I would need to have lost at least one hundred pounds in order to take the lead away and win the grand prize. Knowing I had lost well over that made me feel confident and beside myself with excitement.

I will never forget the mix of emotions that evening as I stepped up to the scale for the final time to win the $250,000 grand prize and the title of *The Biggest Loser* as America cheered me on and confetti shot out to flutter down everywhere and cover us all. Euphoric on the outside, but strangely peaceful on the inside, I had somehow known from the start that it would be my night. Once the confetti started falling, it became a madhouse. Over the next fifteen minutes, I was moved around to give close to twenty-five interviews and had barely hugged my family before I was pulled away from my grandmother and dragged off to a limo with a change of clothes waiting for me. By 8:00 a.m., I was live on the *Today* show with no sleep or makeup change after taking a red-eye to New York. I stayed there for two days of a whirlwind media blitz, including several radio programs and three magazine photo shoots. I'd never had so much fun packed into two days (as exciting as the New York makeover trip was a few months earlier, there had still been a lot of pressure because we weren't finished yet), even though I collapsed in an exhausted heap by the time I made it back home.

Personally, my victory was far beyond anything I could have imagined walking away from my *TBL* experience with. Never again would I go back to living half a life after getting a taste of what my heavenly Father had been trying to offer me all along. The grand prize was wonderful, but the lasting reward was the discovery of who I am when I am thrown into the refiner's fire and the heat is cranked up. I learned so much about myself throughout the entire experience. Although it was a tremendous and pleasant surprise to learn that I am made of much tougher stuff than I realized, and that I am much stronger than I'd thought, the greatest thing that I learned was that I am not alone in the fire—Someone else is in there with me, and He makes all the difference.

It was an unforgettable journey, and I was humbled and overwhelmed by the way God orchestrated everything so perfectly from start to finish. The most wonderful part was that the show's finale wasn't the end of anything—it was the first page of a brand-new chapter, and I couldn't wait to start filling it in.

9

Unscripted Bliss

True love begins when nothing is looked for in return.
—Antoine de Saint-Exupéry, *The Wisdom of the Sands*

The peace I felt amid all the bright lights and chaos of the finale night was not by accident. I knew that night when I stood in front of America—as the crowned champion of *The Biggest Loser*—that I had done much more than put in the work to lose 110 pounds. I'd endured the more difficult process of looking deep inside myself to face the issues that had been holding me back from living a full life. Having unpacked many of those issues while on the ranch, I had a newfound confidence and a more open heart. I was truly ready to go live the life God had so masterfully helped me build. This meant I was ready to accept the love, affection, and grace that I had never felt genuinely worthy of accepting before.

Guess what? Not only had God been at work in my heart restoring the relationship I had with my mom, He had also been opening my heart and my eyes to someone else … someone who had been right in front of me all along. Yes—Micah. This was something I never saw coming, something I never would have imagined. But if there's one other thing I learned during my time on the ranch, it's *never say never.*

God had sown that seed with Micah years before. In the months between coming home from the ranch and the finale—in a new space in time, with a fresh perspective on life—Micah and I would feed and water that seed to help it grow into something truly amazing.

Letters from a Certain Someone

While on campus, letters from home were highly cherished, yet I really didn't expect to get many from people other than my immediate family. After all, I had done a pretty good job of isolating myself from the rest of the world prior to arriving on the ranch. And certainly by the end of our time on *TBL,* everyone's letters from home were getting to be few and far between. So imagine my surprise when one day during the last week on the ranch I received two letters—both postmarked "Plano, Texas." The sender was none other than Micah, the guy who had both annoyed and inspired me in my previous life at the TV network. The one with whom I had forever commemorated our journey to a U2 concert by way of a tattoo on my shoulder that simply said *Adonai*—the Hebrew word for "Lord."

I remember getting Micah's first letter and thinking how predictable it seemed. For one thing, it was typed, not handwritten, and the contents weren't what I would call personal. The message was pretty vanilla—something along the lines of a "Hey, I guess I should write this letter to let you know I hope you are well, but I'm a dude and I don't write letters, so I'll just tell you what's been going on in my world" kind of letter. Even though the first letter was impersonal, it still made me smile as I found myself lost in thoughts that retraced the path that got us both to this place. Here I was … in California … on a reality show … reading a letter from the guy who used to totally annoy me.

When Micah and I worked together, we spent some time as friends and coworkers outside of the office after our trip to Hawaii. Yet the fishbowl environment of our workplace did not foster the cultivation of relationships, but rather was a setting where people felt scrutinized and judged. Because of that, we knew that any thoughts of a deeper personal connection there were out from the start.

Because our job agendas were different, our goals often conflicted (pleasing my boss became my priority; making good TV was his), and we locked horns frequently and often in a public way. Our typical interaction would have pegged us as a very unlikely couple in the sight of our coworkers. But because we both had a high regard for each other's character, a friendship developed. I came to respect and admire Micah as a person, believer, and friend. Although the timing was not good for anything beyond a friendship because of our work situation and all the chaos swirling around in my personal life, I felt a special connection with him despite being emotionally unavailable for anything more.

Back when Micah had quit his job at the TV network, I was at a loss. Although I admired him for leaving, I remember thinking I couldn't believe he actually did it. He wanted something different from life, and he was off to find it. It seemed simple enough, but at the time, I was so driven by my need for security and fear of the unknown that his decision seemed like a blind and reckless leap. Although I was secretly longing to move on myself, I was too fearful to leave the safety of my familiar surroundings, despite my growing unhappiness there.

As I helped Micah pack up his office and sent him on his way, we agreed to keep in touch and to try to see each other soon. Well, "soon" turned into several months. By the time we got around to meeting up for dinner I, too, had found the courage to leave my job and was only about a week away from flying out to California for *TBL*. We had so much to catch up on but so little time. He had heard that I had left the network, and he also knew that I was in a new place emotionally and that the fog that I had been living in was clearing. Our dinner was just enough to leave me wondering "what if?" *What if I come back a changed person from the inside out—could I possibly date Micah?* Our obstacles and reasons for not dating were clearing away one by one, and soon we would get the chance to see if there was anything deeper to pursue together.

As I opened the second letter, I noticed immediately that this one was handwritten. Because Micah is a technology junkie and has every electronic gadget at his fingertips, he could have typed a letter and had it out the door in two shakes. So just the very fact that it was handwritten made it more personal to me. There wasn't anything noteworthy in the content that made it more personal, but it left me feeling that there was a reason why Micah had taken the time to write it by hand. I couldn't help but think it was the sweetest gesture in the world.

Love Is Friendship on Fire

When I got home from *TBL,* where a surprise party of family and friends at my dad's house would welcome me back, Micah was there. We talked briefly and agreed to meet up for coffee later in the week. And I would be lying if I said I wasn't anxious to hang out with him. He had been on my mind a lot since receiving the letters from him that last week on the ranch. I couldn't wait to tell him all about my grand adventure and show him how much I had changed. I was so excited about everything I had been through and learned in just a few short months. Our little coffee "chat" lasted more than three hours, and in that time a friendship was reignited and a romance began blooming. His thoughts and questions were not, "Tell me all about the behind-the-scenes of reality TV," but rather, "Tell me how you've changed and what you have learned from your time away." We were once again on the exact same page. It was a conversation that I previously wasn't sure we could have had, but as we left that day, I knew that everything that had been wrong before was suddenly right. I loved all the ways our lives were different, yet saw more clearly than ever before how we complemented each other so perfectly. That seed God had sown in both our hearts years ago was finally getting what it needed to grow in His light.

Full-Speed Ahead

Since we'd known each other for several years, we were able to fast-forward through much of the "getting to know you" period of typical relationships. I knew his views on marriage and family. We knew that we shared the same values and commitment to God and wanted many of the same things in life. Everything just fell into place in such a natural way, and soon we were seeing each other regularly. What started out as a few text messages and phone calls a day turned into daily treks across the Dallas metro to hang out in person. Fortunately, having a bit of a financial cushion and the full support of my dad allowed me to have some time to myself and not have to return to a nine-to-five job as I prepared for the *TBL* finale, so my situation combined with Micah's freelance work meant we could spend more time together than most couples ever get at the beginning of a relationship.

The day quickly came when Micah texted me to say we should meet to talk about our relationship and the direction we saw it going to find out if we were both on the same page. Would we continue casually dating, or were both of us ready to take it to the next level? I knew where my heart was—I was all in and hoped he was too. We settled on dinner at one of our favorite Italian restaurants and a movie after. Sitting on the patio that afternoon, he didn't waste any time by being unsure about us. He knew exactly what he wanted—he was all in. So there we were, together, on the same page about the direction we wanted this relationship to take.

The feeling of peace I had that day about the love I had for him could not have felt better. Sure, it was all pretty fast, but I'd never dated anyone and had such a settled sense of well-being and peace about it. I could see clearly how my love for him had grown out of a healthy friendship and how all the work I did on the inside during *TBL* learning to trust God's path for me had erased the "what ifs?" that had swirled around in my head before.

All I could think that day as we sat on the patio of the restaurant was that *this* was living. All the grueling work I did during *TBL*—the very work that I'd wanted to run away from when I arrived on campus—had successfully chipped away the armor I had used for so long to protect myself. It was an "unarmoring" that left me confident in myself and strong in my faith and truly ready to jump heart first into a new life with my best friend.

The months breezed past, and we were nearing the *TBL* finale. Things had definitely become quite serious between us. No longer was it a question of *would* we get married, but instead, *when* we would we would get engaged and then married.

I was ready to share my new life with a person who could appreciate my fresh start and who would push me to continue growing in my faith every day. I knew I had found someone who was brave enough to challenge both of us to climb to new heights, yet kind enough to understand and accept my imperfections in a way that would make me feel comforted and loved unconditionally.

Saying Yes!

Christmas was only a few weeks after the finale, and we planned to spend our time together between our families. We would spend Christmas Eve with Micah's family and Christmas morning alone together … just the two of us. Then we would spend the afternoon with my family.

I have been told once or twice that I am hard to buy for. I like to think of it as that I know exactly what I want out of life. Regardless, I felt bad that Micah was so nervous about the first holiday when we would be exchanging gifts. We moved quickly through a gift exchange, and I thought he did a great job, especially for not knowing all the little things it usually takes people years to discover about each other.

I was about to rush off to get ready for the rest of our day when Micah told me there was one more gift hidden in the tree I had missed. I searched and came across a medium-sized blue box. I yelled "Earrings!" as I ripped the bow off and snapped open the Tacori box. My eyes grew wide. *Not earrings!* Even more quickly than I'd opened the box, I slammed it shut and handed it shakily to Micah, who was already on one knee. He fought through tears and, kneeling there, asked me to marry him. Overjoyed, I said yes, and he slipped the ring onto my finger.

As romantic as that moment was, telling my family the news would be much different. "Micah asked me to marry him.... And I said *yes!*" I blurted out at the end of the prayer just before our meal. I had been fidgeting up to that point, pulling my sweater over my hand so they wouldn't see the ring on my finger before I had a chance to make the announcement, but I couldn't wait. I lost control and couldn't help just screaming it out.

My family was thrilled for us, as they respected Micah and knew he was a perfect match for me. We quickly made plans for the wedding so we could begin the next season of life together.

We married in the summer of 2009, just shy of a year from when the seed of a growing friendship blossomed into a romance guided by the hand of God. We wanted our wedding to be symbolic of how we would live our married life—surrounded by family and friends with the feeling being inviting and warm. (And I also mean that literally. We had an outside wedding in Texas in the month of June.) We wanted our special day to feel more like a family reunion for all our guests and less like a stuffy wedding. "Love" was our theme of the day, and I believe we achieved it. It was a magical occasion that just felt right.

Following a honeymoon that took us back to the very place where I first learned to see Micah as not just a coworker but a dear friend—Hawaii—we returned to Texas to begin the rest of our life.

Built to Last

As Micah and I began our journey together as husband and wife, I knew the work we had ahead of us to create a simple yet God-filled marriage would be the most important work of our lives. All the stories of the lives of others we had produced, directed, and edited into nice little five-minute television segments would be nothing compared to the script we were writing of our own lives. For that we would need prayer.

I know being lifted up in prayer by close family and friends has allowed us to grow even stronger with each new day. In particular, I have been so blessed to have one specific encourager and spiritual confidant lifting me up in prayer for many, many years. And when I told her I had fallen in love with Micah and had decided to spend the rest of life with him, it went without saying that she would continue praying for me—for us.

> As for me and my household, we will serve the LORD. (Josh. 24:15)

In December of 2010—roughly a year and a half after Micah and I stood in front of our family and friends and vowed before God to love one another and to grow in Christ until death do us part—I received the sweetest, most encouraging message from this same friend, Cyndy:

> *Getting married, having family, and being connected are all important parts of who you are and*

what you are to share with others. Others need what you have! Others need to know marriage can be amazing! Others need to know that you have to support each other in marriage. Others need to know that family is important.

As I sat in my home office that December morning across from Micah, watching him work, Cyndy's words filled me with tears of joy. She had just validated everything I knew to be true about our commitment to each other and to sharing that commitment with others who needed to know that marriage and family are important.

The timing of Cyndy's words could not have been more perfect. Micah and I had just opened up our home for the week to a friend who was looking to get out of town to recharge after a pretty intense year of transitions in her professional and personal life. Micah and I weren't going to be particularly busy that week anyway, and with both of us having designed our careers to be extremely flexible and based out of our home, entertaining an out-of-town guest for a few days wasn't difficult at all.

For the most part, Micah and I simply lived the life we normally would as if no one was there with us. We included our friend in an outing to see the Dallas Symphony Orchestra play with Michael W. Smith, and she also accompanied us to a public-speaking event I did that week. But for the most part, we just lived life. We played a few board games, we went out for dinner a few times, and attempted to cook some healthy muffins from Jillian's newly released *Master Your Metabolism* cookbook.

The week ended, our friend packed up and went home, and a few days later we got a package in the mail. In it was a replacement for a kitchen gadget that had broken during her stay at our house and a card that simply said, "Thank you for showing me that marriage is special when God is truly front and center. I love you both to bits."

Wow, I thought at the time. *What an incredible compliment!* Micah and I had done nothing out of the ordinary, but it was enough to impress upon our friend that, yes, God is truly front and center in our home. And having been able to impress upon our single friend the importance of God and family made Cyndy's words that day all the more touching. What validation that it's in the little moments when we are just being Micah and Michelle, in unscripted bliss, when these virtues shine through the most.

Neither Micah nor I have a fairy-tale view of marriage or the hard work it takes to have a marriage that is built to last, but it's a commitment we work on every single day. And in the two-plus years we've been married, there have been good days and there have been not-so-good days, but I can honestly say with each new day I am married to him, our love and mutual respect for each other grows.

As I look back now on our beginning and pray about our future, I am simply enjoying our present together. I am beyond grateful that where I am weak he is strong—and that God is at the center of it all.

10

More than I Imagined

*God can do anything, you know—far more than you could
ever imagine or guess or request in your wildest dreams!*
—Ephesians 3:20 (MSG)

Someone much wiser than I am once said if you want to hear God
laugh, go ahead and tell Him your plans. How true that is! My life
post-*TBL* certainly shaped up to be so much different from what
I had ever envisioned it being—so much more than I imagined.
I was the girl who simply thought I'd show up on the ranch, stay
a few weeks, and lose just enough weight to jumpstart my own

weight-loss journey. I also knew the time away with my mom could give us a real opportunity not to "fix" our relationship but to put us both in places that would allow our hearts to begin heal-ing—on a path where we could walk in love toward each other again. I had certainly gotten what I was looking for out of the experience, and my new life with Micah was only one surprising piece of what God had in store for me.

This book has chronicled my struggle to use my voice both before *TBL* and during my time on the ranch. God allowed me to find my voice during the show, and He soon gave me the opportu-nity to use it for His will in a twist that only He could orchestrate.

The Signs Are Everywhere

Not long after I began settling into life after the *TBL* finale in December of 2008, I started noticing billboards with the words *I am Second* as I drove around the Dallas metroplex. I have just enough of an inquisitive side that I was instantly curious and wanted to know what these billboards meant. They were so sim-ple, yet so stunning. The words *I am Second* in a playful white font jumped out against a solid black background and left onlookers intrigued—a true sign of a powerful and effective ad campaign. But what did it mean? Who was second? And beyond that … Who was first?

Soon after, the face of Brian Welch from the '90s grunge band Korn began to surface on these same billboards next to the words. *Aha!* This campaign was obviously ministry driven. I knew

Brian Welch's story of how he climbed out of the abyss of addiction by finding God and leaning on his faith to anchor his now God-filled life. I immediately rushed home and googled *Brian Welch* and *I am Second* and came across one of the most powerful video testimonials I'd ever seen. To say I was blown away would be an understatement—I was absolutely hooked. I wanted to learn everything I could about this campaign. I thought, *How simple this message is, yet such a perfect way to reach the hearts of so many! I am second because God is first.* Certainly I had seen the wonder God worked in my own life when I placed my faith and trust in Him. It was a message that I believed in with every fiber of my soul. And I wanted to be a part of it.

I told Micah about the campaign and my interest in it, not knowing that he was actually doing some freelance work for the ministry behind the campaign. Micah mentioned to someone there that he had recently asked me to marry him and how I couldn't stop talking about this campaign. In an amazing coincidence, one of the people he shared this information with already knew my story because she had worked with my mom at Fellowship Church in Grapevine, Texas. She was thrilled to learn how intrigued I was with their project.

Soon enough, I was sitting in a production studio with one small chair and a tiny light above me telling my story to a camera crew. I was about to become a "Second."

The shoot was unlike anything I'd ever done. After winning *TBL,* I had done the talk-show circuit—*Ellen, Rachael Ray, Today,* and *Larry King Live*—and I'd appeared on dozens of magazine covers. Each time I'd done a cover or a TV interview, the stylists couldn't wait to get their hands on me and play dress up with the girl who had just gone from fat to fit in a matter of months. And I'll fully admit I loved it. I'm a girly girl and a lover of all things fashion. More often than not, you will find me dressed to the nines with the trendiest shoes I can find, along with the flashiest bracelets and the most ginormous watches adorning my arms. After all, they go perfectly with my whiter-than-white smile.

But on this day, I was stripped of all those distractions and instead wore a black T-shirt and no adornments other than my engagement ring and a tiny nylon thread bracelet. This was no coincidence. The campaign is meant to be raw—to capture people in their most basic and simplistic states, stripped away of the material things so that God shines through as the accessory that's noticed first.

I thought back to the night on the ranch when I told God if He could use me to reach people, I would honor His wishes. It was so humbling, especially since I had been given a platform with the *I am Second* campaign to turn people's eyes back to Him, offering up the glory and honor that is rightfully His. It was—in a word—perfect.

It Goes Places I Can't

I think what I love most about being part of the *I am Second* campaign is that it can go places and reach people I physically cannot. This became clear to me during the second anniversary celebration of the campaign. As they brought me out on stage for my interview at Bent Tree Bible Fellowship in Carrollton, Texas, I was joined by a special surprise guest, a Navy SEAL who had come to share a remarkable story in person with me. He explained that he had been stationed overseas and was in charge of the weekly church services for his troops. As part of his presentations, he shared various *I am Second* videos. One week he happened to show the video that featured my story. When the church service concluded, a fellow SEAL came up to him, crying. This other SEAL was the "toughest of the tough," not someone you would have thought capable of tears, let alone crying in front of fellow soldiers. He went on to say that this guy had been struggling with the toll the war had taken on his marriage and just how strained his relationship with his wife had become. He had been considering divorce, and the very night before had pretty much made up his mind that he would end his marriage.

But after seeing my video, he began to think about the situation in a completely different way. For the first time, he took into consideration the effect a divorce would have on his little girl. Because of the experience I shared, he abandoned the idea of leaving his wife and instead planned to call her that very day to let her know they needed to try harder to work through their problems. He was committed to putting God first in their marriage to save it.

The funny thing is, I can remember the day when I taped the interview he saw. Having been surrounded by TV for so long, it sometimes felt like old hat. A taped interview should have been even less stressful than some of the live ones I had done. But on the day of my *I am Second* interview, I was a total wreck. I knew that this video was different, and that I would have to dig deeper than I ever had before in order for it to be as real and honest as I wanted it to be. I remember asking God to speak through my life to show the world how good trusting Him could be. And then I let it all go so He could have His way.

So to see this man standing in front of me on stage, describing the impact my video had somewhere on the other side of the world—for someone who was risking his life to protect mine— was beyond humbling. Everything had come full circle, and I understood what it felt like to be emptied to be filled again.

I could only smile and say, "This is what it's all about." I thanked him for telling his story, for his service, and for being willing to share my video in hopes of reaching his fellow soldiers.

God didn't stop asking me to use my voice for His will with the *I am Second* campaign, and I am grateful that He soon put me on a path to reach thousands of women across America.

Women of Faith

Women of Faith (WOF) is a ministry tour based out of Dallas, Texas, that makes two-day stops in cities around the country. Its purpose is to bring women of all backgrounds together to worship God and grow stronger in their faith through the powerful stories of a panel of amazing women.

So you can imagine how overwhelmed and intimidated I was when Women of Faith first approached me and asked me to tour with them and share my story. I'd always had a high regard for the caliber of the speakers who headlined for the group, and I couldn't imagine being surrounded by such bold and remarkable women of God.

Some of the headliners of the tour included godly women I grew up admiring from afar and never thought I'd have an opportunity to work with side by side. Who would have ever thought I could share a platform with Sheila Walsh, Luci Swindoll, or Lisa Harper? Not me! These women were polished. Their love for Christ and the confidence they displayed when they rose to tell their powerful stories of learning to trust God were both admirable and slightly incomprehensible to me.

Even as I considered joining WOF on the tour, I learned so much about image versus purpose. When I was first presented with this opportunity, old fears came rushing up from deep inside me. Where would my story fit in? Would my story be good enough? Could my message measure up to those of these amazing women? After all, they were seasoned speakers, accomplished authors, and theological geniuses. But God worked on my heart and made me realize that it's never about the messenger. Instead, it's all about the message—I was carrying His message of hope that He had prepared for others who needed to hear it. It wasn't about me at all! With an open heart and no idea what to expect, I signed on the dotted line and officially joined the "Imagine" tour of Women of Faith 2010.

The first stop on the tour took me to Billings, Montana, in springtime, and it was here I got my first glimpse of exactly what I had signed up for: A massive number of women all gathered in a huge arena listening to me bare my soul and share my heart. And while I thought I had resolved the fears of "Would I be good enough?" with God before I signed up for the tour, those emotions flooded my mind again. Not just in Billings, but well into the ten other cities of the tour, I wrestled with those fears over and over and over again.

Call it a God thing, but the format of the event billed me as the last speaker—late in the afternoon on the final day of the event. That meant I would sit and listen to each speaker share her remarkable message with the women before I would get up and share my own. With each stop of the tour, I grew stronger in my own faith and trust in God as I sat and listened to these women teach the Word in ways I had never heard before. The nerves and fear of not being good enough were always erased by the time I hit the stage—allowing me to pour all my strength into truly opening my heart and sharing it with reckless abandon for His will.

Learning to Trust Women Again

The one thing I didn't expect to come from my experience with Women of Faith was the deep respect, admiration, trust, and friendship I built with each and every one of the speakers on the tour. Although my relationship with Jillian had shown me I was capable of trusting women again, my heart was still guarded toward this concept in many ways. But each weekend, as I would show up for another Women of Faith tour date, these women chipped away at that issue by simply being their fabulous selves. They led by example—openly bestowing trust on each other and inspiring it in those around them. Watching them interact as a group and having them accept me with open arms, trusting me with some of their most vulnerable moments, touched my heart in ways I simply cannot express. Never before had I been around so many women filled with such grace and love. It made it impossible for me to keep a wall up, and I felt God working to break down the trust issue I had been holding on to for so many years. In learning to trust these women, I was growing stronger in my trust in God. That has made me a better woman, wife, sister, daughter, and friend. Those women helped build a bridge from the Michelle I had become post-*TBL*—new in my understanding of the power that comes with fully trusting God—to the Michelle I'm still becoming, the Michelle who shares a little more of my heart and trusts with a little more ease every single day.

Teachable Moments

I'm a firm believer in teachable moments. I want to always stay open and present so that I never miss an opportunity to learn. When Jesus chided Martha about her busywork during His visit to her home, He was not saying we should all live like slobs and forget housework. What He was emphasizing, and what we need to remind ourselves of daily, is our need to watch for the opportunities that come to us that are worth setting aside the daily toil. It is simply about recognizing those "God moments" that change us and teach us and leave us forever different. Mary knew her priorities, and Jesus defended her choice to spend time with Him rather than lose a moment of His divine presence. We should never be so busy with our own "stuff" that we fail to recognize the important lessons presented to us.

My time on the Women of Faith tour was full of teachable moments, and for that I am eternally grateful. God placed me in an environment to learn from the very best about how to share my faith in a way that could make a profound impact on the lives of others. Getting that firsthand experience of Women of Faith made me want to share this unique event with every woman I knew. I kept my eyes open for any opportunity to invite my friends and even complete strangers. That intention would lead to an unexpected teachable moment for a dear friend—and another opportunity for me to thank God while I put my trust in Him.

During the 2010 tour, Sheila Walsh shared an incredibly inspirational testimony about the power of learning to trust God even in one's darkest hour. She openly shared the story of her emotional breakdown, time spent in a mental health facility, and journey back to better emotional health and an even stronger relationship with God. Each week she shared this story, it was as if I were hearing it for the first time. I'm not sure what it was about her testimony that spoke to me and touched my soul so deeply, but it made me want to deepen my commitment to fully trust God—to learn to truly allow Him to be the ultimate Shepherd in my life. The more I sat and pondered the idea, the more I wanted to put it into practice. I became even more eager to share my newfound wisdom with anyone willing to listen.

I wouldn't have to wait long. About the same time I began touring with Women of Faith and listening to Sheila's story week after week, a dear friend of mine began her own struggle with learning to trust God in her darkest hour. She had a sister who had spent time over the past year seeking treatment in an inpatient mental health facility for major trauma that left her on the brink of suicide. When I spoke with my friend, I could tell the role she was playing as her sister's advocate was growing very tiring for her. It's not shocking that I would spot this sort of John Wayne role, given my history of playing that very same role to my own family for so many years. I wasn't sure exactly where my friend stood in her faith, and honestly I didn't really care. I just knew she needed to hear Sheila's message—and all the better if her sister could hear it too. I searched for a tour stop close to where her family lived and quickly reserved tickets for her, her sister, and their mom.

Much to my delight, all three of them showed up. I think my friend thought I wanted her to hear my talk—but my motivation wasn't about getting her to the arena to hear me. I knew God had bigger plans than that. But in an ironic twist, when it came time for Sheila to share her testimony of her time in a mental health facility, I looked over and saw my friend and her mother, but not her sister. Apparently she wasn't feeling well and had remained at the hotel to rest in hopes of feeling better in time to catch my talk later that afternoon. I wasn't concerned because I put my trust in the fact that God still got the powerful message to my friend, and I knew it would be enough. After Sheila's talk, my friend rushed over to where I sat with the other speakers and said, in a panic, "Michelle, I can't believe my sister wasn't here to listen to this! I'm so bummed!" This was my clue that the seed had been planted in my friend. What I didn't know is how quickly she would need to turn around and share that message with her sister.

The Monday after this particular weekend, I got a phone call in the middle of the afternoon from my friend. She sounded eerily calm when I asked her how things were going, and she casually said, "Michelle, I'm on the way to pick up my sister to check her back into the mental health facility. She called me this morning and is struggling emotionally again and is saying she doesn't want to live any longer. I'm simply calling for two reasons. One, I'm asking for your prayers, and two, I can't remember the name of that Sheila Walsh book that chronicles her own battle with depression, and I want to make sure my sister has a copy so she can begin reading it during her stay at the hospital."

This sort of calm behavior isn't uncommon for my friend. She is very much the rock when it comes to her family and tends to internalize most of her own pain. But I wasn't worried about her internalizing *this* pain; I knew exactly what she was doing. She was putting into practice what she had learned just two days earlier at Women of Faith about the power of trusting God. She didn't call crying and desperate, and she wasn't trying to play John Wayne and save her sister. Instead, she was choosing to release that burden and become a sheep in God's pasture by placing her faith in Him and asking for prayers that both she and her sister would find inner peace in that moment of chaos. And she believed enough in Sheila's message that she wanted her sister to read it. My teachable moment of learning to trust God had been passed on to my friend, and in that one phone call, I realized the impact that Women of Faith was having on my world.

I've seen a visible shift in my friend since that weekend at Women of Faith. And while my friend still battles with her struggle of finding the balance of learning to trust God, I know her walk with Him grows stronger every single day.

Bring on the Huggers

If you have never been hugged by the likes of Luci Swindoll, Sheila Walsh, Lisa Harper, Lisa Whelchel, or any of the other amazing Women of Faithers, I suggest you get yourself to the next stop on the WOF tour because I promise you won't be disappointed. I've never been around so many women in the same space who can hug so freely and expect nothing in return. Hugs happen frequently with these women, and what an amazing feeling it was every time they extended their arms to me—to offer a shoulder to cry on if I was having a bad day or simply to acknowledge my presence in a room. There wasn't a moment on the tour when hugs were off-limits, and they flowed easily between us all. Having learned to keep people at such a distance for so long, the fact that I *wanted* to hug these women—that I would literally run across an arena to hug them—meant the world to me and made me proud.

I have such gratitude to them for allowing me to see that I'm wide open and ready for huggers in my life. More importantly, I'm not just ready for hugs—I *need* them. I understand more deeply than ever before the power of human touch, and I hug with everything in me. And I'm just going to warn you now—there's a pretty good chance that I will hug you should we ever meet in public. I'm officially a hugger these days, and I like it that way!

Reliving the Pain, One Tour Date at a Time

Women of Faith would also serve as a test of the commitment I made to God on the night I lay in my bed at the ranch, crying out to Him and promising I would love my mom right where she was. Each week as I began to share my story with the crowds at Women of Faith, I would feel the pain of my parents' divorce and my mom's decision to leave me behind. I wasn't prepared for the pain I would experience as I retold the story each week, and I began to question whether or not I had truly forgiven her. There I would be, standing onstage, speaking to thousands of women, retelling the story of my mom leaving me and the painful journey of the years that followed, and I would begin to sob as the hurt of the past came front and center for me to deal with all over again. As I wrestled with navigating this gut-wrenching pain onstage, and also trying to remain raw and real for the people who had come to hear my story and be moved by it, I would start to think, *Michelle, are you* really *the person you say you are now? Have you*

truly forgiven Mom, and are you really ready and willing to love her
right where she is in this moment?

Some dates on the tour were tougher than others as I began
to realize the walk in forgiveness, grace, and love with my mom
wouldn't be easy. And it was in these moments I felt the overwhelming urge to run directly toward Him and share my struggle
with Him. What a contrast to the way I wanted to run *away* from
Him in my pre-*TBL* days! He continued to show me that He had
His hand on my heart and that my belief in Him would see me
through. And it did.

Common Ground

The very public journey to nurse Mom's and my broken relationship back to health has at times come with an unexpected level
of pressure. I could never have predicted the number of people
who have expressed to Mom and I their need to know what has
become of us and the new relationship we agreed to forge while
on the ranch. So many fans with very caring hearts have—with
the very best of intentions—cast their own expectations on us as
to what that relationship should look like at this point.

And this is what I want to share with everyone about what the
journey with my mom looks like: I've learned to keep it simple.
For the first time since the divorce, I found some common ground
through our *Biggest Loser* experience, and I have made a very con-
scious effort to build our relationship from that place. So staying
as transparent as possible and allowing the healing process to

unfold naturally keeps me from feeling as if I have to control it or that I have to see certain markers as proof of progress. Laying it all before God on a daily basis and allowing Him to be the captain of my ship has freed me of the weight of expectations I once placed on myself and those the outside world placed on me.

One thing that has stuck with me since that phone call nearly ten years ago was that Mom told me I'd understand when I was older. Well, I'm definitely older, and while there is still plenty in life that I don't understand, one thing is certain: I understand that my mom, like all of us, is a unique person—someone who could not (and should not) be molded into my vision of who she should be, whether I am eighteen or twenty-eight. I have come to accept that, like every other person on this earth, including me, my mom isn't perfect and will make mistakes. The mom I needed at eighteen is not the mom I need today. Today, I can accept a friendship with my mom that is focused on moving forward. Knowing that our past issues will never be erased but also that they will no longer be able to hold my heart hostage has brought me to a new place of maturity and acceptance. I will never be immobilized from moving forward again, and I will never again let six years go by without sitting down to talk.

What may not be enough for some people works well for us as we walk through the days God has graciously given us together. Although I would never lead you to believe that our relationship is perfectly healed, it's the truth of where we are right now, and further than we ever could have imagined we'd be just a few short years ago. I have comfort and peace in knowing that every day I walk in grace with her is an opportunity for God to do something new in our lives together. We are a true picture of "becoming," and we embrace the awkward and messy parts because they represent the beauty of change, acceptance, and most of all, fearlessness of what is yet ahead.

11

True Reality

Go confidently in the direction of your dreams. Live the life you've imagined.

—Henry David Thoreau, paraphrase from *Walden*

When I signed up for *The Biggest Loser,* I knew that losing the weight I had gained would be only half the battle. It would indeed be a great bonus—I would have a new body at the end of the day. But I didn't fool myself into thinking that food had ever been my real problem, or that a brand-new body would cure the hurt that existed deep inside my soul. I knew the physical weight I put on after my mother left was simply the most visible symptom of my secret pain of struggling to find my place in this world and my own voice. I knew I would have to change from the inside out in order to shed the *emotional* weight necessary before I could truly move forward with a new purpose-filled life. It's been some of the hardest work I've ever done, but it's also been the most rewarding because I've come out on the other side with a renewed relationship with God and the hope of a more honest way of living. New doors of understanding have been opened to me, friendships have been mended, and relationships deepened. I've tasted the freedom that fearlessness offers, and I simply have no desire to go back to the half life based on fear that I used to live.

Respecting the Two Pounds

Despite the excitement of losing so much weight and winning *TBL,* I realized even before the show's final week that a "new me" was emerging that had nothing to do with the scale. Back in week two, when I had lost two pounds, host Alison Sweeney gave me a look of pity following my weigh-in and said, "Michelle, it must be difficult to see only two pounds on the board."

I didn't even blink an eye in my response. Yes, it was difficult. Yes, I had worked very hard that week, more than two pounds' worth. But they were two pounds off my body that I would never see again. I was not upset at the numbers because I had fully earned those two pounds. I finished by saying I respected those two pounds, and that the numbers may have been low but my spirit was high.

Alison seemed a bit surprised, but that was my way of saying that I refuse to allow the scale to define me, even in the midst of a game driven by numbers. The bigger picture—the process that was taking place in my head and in my heart that was truly changing me from the inside out—had always been more important than the yellow line (the one demarcating the two players with the lowest weight loss that week and at risk of being voted off the ranch). I was playing for far greater stakes than numbers on a scale. Even today, as long as I remind myself on a regular basis what my life's priorities are, I know I will never again fall victim to the anxiety and insecurities that so many of us struggle with as we try to live up to the expectations of a harsh and demanding world.

The Bible reminds us in Zechariah 4:10 to not despise the day of small beginnings. All of our efforts are valuable, and we are meant to focus on where we are going rather than where we may find ourselves at any moment in this up-and-down world in which we live.

Let's be clear: Staying connected to our physical health and well-being is an important part of living a full life. Since leaving the ranch and settling into my true reality, I have the power to choose my message. And I have intentionally chosen not to be a part of any program or campaign that reduces people to numbers and forces them to focus all their efforts to fix the outside when, in almost every case, they are broken on the inside. That was my own story for too many years, so it is especially important for me to speak up on the issue of hiding behind false perfection at the expense of living an honest life. I want to encourage people to respect their two pounds and celebrate progress whether it is an inch or a mile at a time.

On this note, I want to share a very personal story that touched my heart—broke it, actually—while I was in Austin, Texas, on a speaking engagement for the Texas Round-Up, a statewide wellness initiative whose mission is to improve the health of all Texans by raising awareness of obesity. I met an remarkable woman who had just gone through an incredible body transformation of her own, yet here she was fighting through tears as she told me her story of how her success was slipping away from her one pound at a time. Understandably, she had become quite the local celebrity for her success in diligently losing the extra weight, but now she suddenly found herself struggling to keep the weight off. Her work schedule had picked up, and that's when the real challenge began—learning to live with her exercise and nutrition program in the real world, with all the chaos and stress that comes with it. She was distraught at losing some of the ground she had fought for and having her dream trampled under the realities of daily living. Her state of despair broke my heart.

I told this woman—who at this point felt defeated and hopeless—that she was one step closer to success now that she knew what didn't work. I encouraged her to take a step back and examine where she believed the major obstacles were so she could revise whichever areas she needed to and respect her two pounds.

Forgive Yourself, Make Course Corrections, and Move On

There are times in life when you are running and leaping with strength and energy. Other times, you find yourself at a slow-paced walk. And there are still other times when it's all you can do to crawl. Whichever situation you find yourself in, just keep moving forward. Over the long haul, your pace is not nearly as important as your direction.

When I found myself on that tiny, swaying platform high in the air during the "leap of faith" challenge, I was terrified. My mind shut down, and nothing seemed to function as it should. But in the middle of the storm that was paralyzing me, I finally found the strength to get up and step out. Yes, it was a half hour later, but that didn't matter. Yes, the cast and crew were down there waiting for me, probably annoyed since we should have wrapped already and been on our way back to the ranch, but that didn't matter either. What mattered was that I finally pushed back against the invisible wall that had always closed in on me, and the most amazing thing happened the moment I touched it. It disappeared! I rose shakily to my feet and—blinded by tears—did nothing but focus on moving forward. As I took that ungainly step off the top of the pole, there was a sudden release and rush of freedom such as I'd never felt before.

I'm sure that most of the people standing there watching the event that day completely missed what was taking place. Looking up and seeing a girl sitting there and trembling in terror for almost thirty minutes would easily qualify as failure and be written off as defeat in most books. Yet it was one of a handful of truly defining moments at the ranch as I overcame a life's worth of fear-based paralysis.

It's easy to get bogged down in a bad moment or by a choice we have made that works against our overall goals. While learning to forgive my mom was at the top of my list, learning to forgive myself and accept the ups and downs of my life has proved just as important. There was a time when I did not know how to stop the slide downward after a slip, but I've learned to catch myself right after the fall so I can do damage control and minimize my recovery time. I don't want a bad moment to become a bad week or a bad month or a bad six years. So when I slip up (as we all do), I have had to learn to forgive myself and move forward. Whether it's about food—having some cake at a birthday party is not the end of the world—or losing ground in the healthy habits I learned in my communication skills, I know I can get up tomorrow and do a better job in any area I may have stumbled in today. And I will continually remind myself of the successes I have already achieved.

Victory is personal. It's not about how something appears or if it meets the criteria for someone else's idea of success, since no one knows exactly where anyone else is on this journey through life. Instead, it is what we receive from any given experience that we master and use as a tool for future challenges that assures that we will keep moving forward, even when we stumble.

Not Really Reality

As I've traveled across the country since my season of *TBL* wrapped, my heart often breaks when people from all walks of life come up to me frustrated they can't lose five, ten, or fifteen pounds a week as they see on the show. It's the unfortunate "unintended consequences" of a show that's meant to inspire people to go out and live their best lives—not mimic the lives of the contestants on the ranch. Season after season contestants come to the ranch and overcome obstacles they never thought possible—showing that, in a world where excuses are around every corner, success can be achieved against all odds.

Trying to use it for anything more than that, or comparing your own scale's results to the numbers that appear each week on the *Loser* scale, will only lead to a sense of inadequacy and hopelessness as you find you just can't duplicate those numbers in a world where people have real-life distractions, daily career obligations, and family responsibilities. Overall, the show's success is based on a training environment that only a few hundred people in the world will ever truly experience, but it has inspired hundreds of thousands of people to not only begin but achieve their own weight-loss goals—and that is its purpose at the end of the day. "Respecting your two pounds" will create an atmosphere of self-acceptance that will ultimately be the solid foundation needed to build your own success.

Finding Balance

If you had asked me to define balance before I left for *The Biggest Loser*, I would have said that balance was the ability to juggle a career in television while also taking care of my entire family—without feeling so tired that I wanted to crawl under the covers and sleep for days on end. Prior to embarking on this journey, I truly thought that to be my best self and lead a balanced life I had to be all things to all people—and if I couldn't do that while also sporting the perfect outfit with perfectly styled hair and makeup and a perfect smile on my face, that somehow I had failed at finding balance.

Thank God I was wrong.

Now I define balance in a much healthier way, which is to say I cherish every moment of life by surrounding myself with people I love and feeling good about who I am—knowing that when I need to be filled or replenished that I am connected to my faith. Leaning on that faith is where balance exists for me.

Coming home after the finale, I will admit finding balance in my life was much harder than I anticipated. I had spent the better part of that previous year in a world where exercising eight hours a day and eating 1,200 calories of extremely healthy food was my norm. When I found myself eating Sprinkles' cupcakes and chips and salsa and going for thirty-minute walks, it simply didn't fit my idea of finding balance in my journey to better health.

Prior to *TBL,* my relationships were out of balance too, and coming home proved to be a challenge as I spent time evaluating what and who was important to me. This ongoing process hasn't been an easy one, but I know in my heart my life is better for it and more balanced than ever before.

Finding balance has allowed new friendships to flourish and old friendships to be renewed and restored. I was at lunch the other day marveling at the fact that I can now sit, have a meal, and not think constantly in the back of my mind that I am being judged based on how I look, or that I have to smile all the time no matter what I may be feeling inside. My search for balance has simplified my life—I just sat and enjoyed the company of my friend, whom I no longer had to look at with two sets of eyes— one set as my boss and the other as my best friend. I only needed to see her as my friend. It was the most precious feeling to see the new place my friend was also walking in, knowing that God had restored both our lives, and as a small miracle even restored a friendship that I thought was lost.

Construction Ahead

I live in Grapevine, Texas, not far from the Dallas-Fort Worth airport. My home sits near a highway that connects two other major roadways in the Dallas metroplex that have been under construction since Jesus was a baby. (OK, not that long, but it seems like an eternity. Truly.) With the construction has come hours of delay for the daily commuters, and each day these commuters wait for the construction to ease up and allow traffic to flow smoothly again. It's as if they have the patience of Job because they understand eventually the construction will make their path much smoother and much safer. Just a few days ago, I was driving this route when I suddenly noticed traffic was finally flowing smoothly in the once-crowded construction zone. The ease with which the traffic flowed that day resonated in my soul. I believe God placed this real-life metaphor in front of me to show me all He had done in my life.

No, I'm not talking about making my commute to Nordstrom Rack or Central Market quicker and less frustrating. (Although, I won't lie, that's not entirely awful because, *hello,* I'm a shopper!)

I'm talking about how smoothly my life flows when I patiently wait for God to construct a new path on my commute. In a real road-construction situation, I would never get out of my car when traffic is backed up, walk over to the foreman of the crew, and ask if I can help make the road so that it all moves more quickly. Yet I found myself doing just that with God in my past when He was trying to repair me. Construction sites have caution cones and broken pavement and heavy equipment I'm not qualified to operate. I must have looked just as out of place trying to make repairs on myself all those years.

When I put my trust in Him and have patience in Him as the foreman of my life—the One who is repairing a broken relationship with my mom, building me a stronger and healthier body, and assembling healthier friendships and a marriage with a solid foundation—I live a life with much fewer obstructions on my ultimate commute to becoming fearless. And I trust that God has made the plans to finish the good work He has already begun. He will continue constructing the life He knows I'm meant to lead as I travel freely in my journey of "becoming."

Finding Inspiration from You

My life of becoming fearless has been filled with incredible opportunities to travel the country meeting people like you who also have inspirational stories to tell. If I had another sixty thousand words, I would dedicate them to telling your stories of triumph against all odds—your own stories of little girl lost to champion crowned.

The stories that you write on my Facebook wall or send me via email at 3:00 a.m. all touch my heart in their own unique ways. Rest assured I read every single one of them and find inspiration in them. Thank you for lifting me up in your prayers at night and thank you for being my biggest fan. The strength I've drawn from your support both during my time on *The Biggest Loser* and since beginning a new journey after the show has no doubt enriched my life in ways I cannot fully express.

My words to each of you, although completely inadequate, are simple and heartfelt: Go live a purposeful, authentic, God-filled life. Don't get so caught up in the "after" that you forget how to "become," or why you started your journey to a better you in the first place. You have the ability to face your fears and live the life you never thought possible. Go live life. God will be patiently waiting as you find out what becoming fearless means in your own story.

The Weight of the World: A Letter to You from Michelle

It's late—really late—and I am writing because I know of no other way to get this out of my heart and into yours. It's funny how God deals with me and my thoughts in the middle of the night. No TV to distract me, no phone or computer looking for my attention. My thoughts tonight are simple: I want you to know more than anything else that you are not alone.

Whether you are struggling with your weight or any other issue that feels as if it might pull you under and bury you alive, I promise you're not the only one out there dealing with the fallout such pain creates. The feelings I personally seem to keep revisiting are failure, doubt, and fear.

Yes, I was the winner of *The Biggest Loser,* a reality show that measures your success based on the percentage of weight lost over a certain number of weeks. I am now a few years past the victory of the show and have since married and am living the life that I at one point thought was just a dream.

Signing up for *TBL* was an extreme way to go about dealing with my weight, and I've since realized how much harder it is to maintain it than it was to lose it. On the show, life is structured and there is a predictable routine to keep you in check. And if that doesn't work, there are always the cameras watching everything you do or the zealous trainers pushing you physically beyond all limits you once believed held you back. So losing weight is the norm.

It is in this part of my life, in the aftermath of the show, that I now lie awake wondering how in the world I am going to get up tomorrow and do this all over again. I thought the transition between a mind-set of working out six to eight hours a day to working out one hour a day like the rest of the world would be an easy one. It wasn't. You see, I struggle with wrapping my brain around one hour being good enough, and if I can't work out six to eight hours a day (who can?) as I did while on the show, I somehow think, *What's the point?* I've recently been able to find a healthier balance with this struggle and try to walk with my mom on most days. It feels good to have found that balance—but it didn't come easy, for sure.

There are times people ask me the one question no one would dream of asking any other woman on the planet: What do you weigh? Sometimes I'm asked for background for a magazine article, sometimes for a story on the Internet, and other times by people I meet in passing. My first thought when I hear this question is, *Answering that question says nothing about the person I am or the person I'm becoming.* But then I remember that it's different for me because I won a reality weight-loss show, and for thirteen weeks America watched me jump on a scale in a sports bra and spandex with my weight on display for all to see. And no matter how I attempt to move on in life, the question will probably always follow me everywhere I go.

And here is the answer I give: Now that I am no longer on TV, what I weigh on any given day is between me and my bathroom scale.

The number on the scale is a funny thing. I have come to terms with it no matter what it is. I don't feel it is something to be ashamed of whether it's up or down, because I've learned it is merely a tool, a way to gauge where I am at any given time. Do I want to live my life at this number? Am I happy, or do I feel sluggish and know I need to hit the gym?

With all the scrutiny that comes with reality television, I can't help but think that some people are waiting to hear bad news. That when the numbers are up I am in some way a failure, and perhaps that makes these people feel better about themselves.

This is the part of the experience that I failed to see coming: the maintenance of everyday life and the examination of every decision. We live in a world filled with temptations, and our lives are fast paced and demanding. People, you and I included, throw "perfect" routines out the window all the time. So here is the reality: I no longer live at my finale weight. But wait—if you think I am declaring defeat with that statement, I am not. Because of the struggles I've faced and overcome, I have a quiet strength and comfort in knowing that I can do whatever it is that I set out to accomplish. I don't get lost easily when it comes to my identity—I know what defines me, and it's not the numbers on my scale.

I have no idea what you will think when you read that statement. What I want you to know is that if you can relate, you're not alone. Really, your life and my life are not very different. Sure, we live miles apart and probably have different family dynamics, but we are very much the same. I am learning that struggling is not something to be ashamed of. It is simply the mark of someone who is still alive.

This knowledge empowers me to press on and move forward, reminding me that I am worth the effort every day. Some days are strong, others not so much. I have learned a lot about forgiveness on many fronts—to forgive myself for the failed perfect meal or the skipped workout or an opportunity I missed in anything from a conversation to a spiritual lesson. And the funny thing about forgiveness is that with it comes the right mind-set to move forward and start again tomorrow without unnecessary guilt.

We can't live if we feel guilty at every turn. So I choose to forgive myself when I need to, and I move on. Sure, I'd love to be that person whose life is so busy that they just forget to eat, but I know that is not who I am at heart. I love life and I love food. Food is more than fuel to me—to most everyone on this planet I believe—and I don't think that's a bad thing. In fact, I think finding balance with my approach to food is very healthy.

Part of me does wonder if tomorrow when I read this letter I will feel a little like Jerry Maguire attempting to write a thought-provoking mission statement that, despite my intentions, will turn into something much different from what I intend to convey, and I will again be the odd man out. But at this very moment,

I don't care. All I know is that if I feel this way, there must be someone else out there experiencing this too, and the last thing I want you to feel is alone.

Setting aside the issue of weight for a moment, you have to look at your motivation. Don't worry, that's the easy part. We can all look to things and people to motivate us to get the weight off. But I urge you to look at *your* life—and yes, write down what your motivation is, but also write down what it is you are willing to sacrifice to get to your goal. I have come to realize that you can have goals and be motivated and, without sacrifice, still get nowhere.

Knowing up front that there will be sacrifices is the realistic way to get to the other side of your struggle, whatever it may be. I encourage you to seek God throughout your journey, and I promise I will be doing the same.

God's best,

Michelle

Notes

1. Parts of this line are from Hillsong, "Desert Song," *This Is Our God* (Sydney, Australia: Hillsong Music Australia, 2008), www.songlyrics.com/hillsong/desert-song-lyrics/.

2. Kevin Fields, "Which City Really Does Have the Most Restaurants Per Capita?" *Article Alley,* November 23, 2006, www.articlealley.com/article_108023_26.html.

3. Eagles, "Hotel California," *Hotel California* (Miami and Los Angeles: Asylum, 1976), www.metrolyrics.com/hotel-california-lyrics-the-eagles.html.

4. Anne Radmacher, quoted in Shelia Murray Bethel, *A New Breed of Leader* (New York: Berkley, 2009), 221.

Bible Resources